Florida Hurricanes and Tropical Storms, 1871–2001

Expanded Edition

John M. Williams and Iver W. Duedall

University Press of Florida

Gainesville · Tallahassee · Tampa · Boca Raton
Pensacola · Orlando · Miami · Jacksonville · Ft. Myers

07 06 05 04 03 02   6 5 4 3 2 1

Library of Congress Cataloging-in-Publication Data
Williams, John M. (John Mills)
Florida hurricanes and tropical storms, 1871–2001 / John M. Williams
and Iver W. Duedall.—Expanded ed.
p. cm.
Rev. ed. of: Florida hurricanes and tropical storms. c. 1997.
Includes bibliographical references and indexes.
ISBN 0-8130-2494-3 (p.: alk. paper)
1. Hurricanes—Florida—History. I. Duedall, Iver W. II. Williams, John M.
(John Mills). Florida hurricanes and tropical storms. III. Title.
QC945.W55 2002
551.55'2'09759—dc21 2001043718

The University Press of Florida is the scholarly publishing agency for the State
University System of Florida, comprising Florida A&M University, Florida Atlantic
University, Florida Gulf Coast University, Florida International University, Florida
State University, University of Central Florida, University of Florida, University of
North Florida, University of South Florida, and University of West Florida.

University Press of Florida
15 Northwest 15th Street
Gainesville, FL 32611–2079
http://www.upf.com

Contents

List of Tables, Figures, and Tracking Plates   vii

Foreword   ix

Preface   xi

1. Introduction   1

2. Florida's Hurricane History   6

    1871–1900   7

    1901–1930   11

    1931–1960   18

    1961–1990   27

3. Four Years and Billions of Dollars Later, 1991–1994   41

4. Allison to Roxanne, 1995   52

5. The Hurricane Seasons of 1996 and 1997   59

6. The Hurricane Season of 1998   62

7. The Hurricane Season of 1999   65

8. The Hurricane Seasons of 2000 and 2001   67

Appendix 1. Hurricane Preparedness   71

Appendix 2. Glossary   76

References   79

Internet References   83

Tables   85

Figures   101

Tracking Plates   143

Index of Named Florida Hurricanes   159

Subject Index   161

About the Authors   168

Section of color plates follows page 82.

Tables, Figures, and Tracking Plates

Tables

1. Saffir/Simpson Scale for classifying hurricanes   85
2. Hurricane classification prior to 1970   86
3. Number of hurricanes, tropical storms, and combined total storms   87
4. Florida hurricanes, 1871–2000   88

Figures

1.A–I.   The Great Miami Hurricane, 1926   101–6
2.A–B.   Damage in Palm Beach, 1928 hurricane   107
3.A–D.   Great Labor Day Hurricane, 1935   108–10
4.A–C.   Hurricane Donna, 1960   111–12
5.   Hurricane Cleo, 1964   113
6.A–B.   Hurricane Betsy, 1965   114–15
7.A–C.   Hurricane David, 1979   116–17
8.   Hurricane Elena, 1985   118
9.A–C.   Hurricane Juan, 1985   119–20
10.A–B.   Hurricane Kate, 1985   121
11.A–I.   Hurricane Andrew, 1992   122–26
12.A–C.   Tropical Storm Alberto, 1994   127–28
13.   Tropical Storm Beryl, Florida Panhandle, 1994   129
14.A–C.   Hurricane Gordon, Florida, 1994   130–31
15.A–B.   Hurricane Allison, 1995   132–33
16.A–E.   Hurricane Erin, 1995   134–36
17.   Tropical Storm Jerry, 1995   137
18.A–E.   Hurricane Opal, 1995   138–40
19.   Five 1995 storms: Jerry, Iris, Karen, Humberto, and Luis   141
20.A–B.   Damage from Hurricane Georges, 1998   142

Color Plates (following page 82)

1. Hurricane Andrew, 1992
2. Hurricane Gordon, 1994
3. Hurricane Allison, 1995
4. Hurricane Erin, 1995
5. Tropical Storm Jerry, 1995
6–7. Hurricane Opal, 1995
8. Tropical Storm Josephine, 1996
9. Hurricane Lili, 1996
10–11. Hurricane Danny, 1997
12. Hurricane Earl, 1998
13–15. Hurricane Georges, 1998
16–17. Hurricane Mitch, 1998
18–19. Hurricane Dennis, 1999
20–21. Hurricane Floyd, 1999
22. Tropical Storm Harvey, 1999
23–25. Hurricane, Irene, 1999
26. Hurricane Helene, 2000
27–28. Tropical Storm Leslie, 2000
29. Tropical Storm Barry, 2001
30. Hurricane Gabrielle, 2001
31. Hurricane Michelle, 2001
32. Final tracks, 2001 season

Tracking Plates

1. 1871–1880   144
2. 1881–1890   145
3. 1891–1900   146
4. 1901–1910   147
5. 1911–1920   148
6. 1921–1930   149
7. 1931–1940   150
8. 1941–1950   151
9. 1951–1960   152
10. 1961–1970   153
11. 1971–1980   154
12. 1981–1990   155
13. 1991–2000   156
14. 2001   157

Foreword

These days, nothing can escape the watchful, high-tech eyes of the National Weather Service. Our satellites and newly installed Doppler radars can detect even the slightest weather system, where it is, and what it is doing.

Public awareness, a problem in the past, has increased also. Hurricane Andrew in 1992 taught a bitter lesson to many whose attitude was apathetic, and it is possible that apathy kills more people than do winds and surges during a hurricane.

With our sophisticated detection and warning equipment, there is no reason for anyone to die because of a hurricane—but people still do. Damage will continue to be proportional to the amount of coastal building, but that can also be controlled.

Evidence showed that communities built away from the water's edge survived serious damage when Hurricane Opal struck the Florida Panhandle in 1995. Homes that followed the local building codes also fared better than those that did not. Some buildings built to code were heavily damaged during Andrew, but Andrew was an exception to the rule. Dr. Theodore Fujita, an expert on severe weather and resulting damage, once suggested that we should build to the 200 mph standard instead of the present 115 mph ratings. But he indicated that costs would be prohibitive, and he was right. So what's the answer?

My next tropical cyclone will be my thirty-fourth, and I have observed several things during those storms. (1) There should be a restriction on how close to the water's edge any type of buildings can be built. (2) Strict adherence to an updated building code should become standard practice; at present it is not. (3) Public awareness should be increased. (4) Perhaps a little test on hurricanes and other storms should be required for future builders and for all present and future homeowners. And (5) evacuation is a necessity in certain areas and should become a precise procedure. Evacuation saves lives!

Those people who are lucky enough to live on our beautiful Florida beaches experience the ultimate in living—but not during a hurricane. They will likely be in an evacuation area and should go at first notice. Owners of mobile homes should expect to move to shelters. Some in other areas will have to move, too. Yes, it is a pain. And it must be a traumatic experience to come back after a storm and find your property inundated and dwellings either destroyed or badly damaged. But in most cases it is possible to reclaim the property and rebuild the dwellings. On the other hand, if you choose to stay, it might be extremely difficult to erase your name from the obituary list.

John M. Williams

Preface

This book presents a summary of the hurricanes and tropical storms that have affected Florida's more than 1,200 miles of coastline during the 130 years from 1871 through 2001.

Prior to publication of the first edition, *Florida Hurricanes and Tropical Storms, 1871–1993: An Historical Survey,* the only books or reports exclusively on Florida hurricanes were R. W. Gray's report, revised by Grady Norton in 1949, titled *Florida Hurricanes,* and a survey by Gordon E. Dunn and the staff of the National Hurricane Center (NHC), also titled *Florida Hurricanes.*

Grady Norton and Gordon Dunn were important figures during the early years of what is now known as the Tropical Prediction Center, formerly the National Hurricane Center. Many considered Grady Norton to be one of the best hurricane forecasters. After his death in 1954, Gordon Dunn was named director of the NHC, and when Gordon retired Dr. Robert Simpson became NHC director. He was followed by Dr. Neil Frank, then Dr. Robert Sheets, and Dr. Robert Burpee, who was the first director of the new facility on the campus of Florida International University in Miami. Stepping in after Dr. Burpee was Jerry Jarrell, and the director of the NHC as of 2001 is Max Mayfield.

In addition to the report *Florida Hurricanes,* the 1997 NHC report titled *The Deadliest, Costliest, and Most Intense United States Hurricanes of This Century* provides invaluable information on both historical and recent hurricanes affecting Florida and other parts of the United States.

Our primary goals in preparing this revised edition were to update the historical work as it pertains to Florida, to consolidate and standardize technical terms published at the beginning of each hurricane season on hurricane tracking maps, and to introduce new material pertaining to Florida: a detailed historical discussion, a chronological listing of all Florida hurricanes, 14 plates of hurricane and tropical storm tracks grouped into 10-year increments, 32 colored images of tropical cyclones, and a table showing the number of tropical storms and hurricanes by 10-year increments. The book is written on a nontechnical level for the general reader who is interested in knowing when and where tropical cyclones have affected Florida and the magnitude of damage inflicted by the storms. Those wanting more technical information on tropical cyclones can consult the references, contact the NHC directly, or visit the National Hurricane Center website (see Internet References).

Principal reference documents used in preparing this book, in addition to the ones already mentioned, were the 1999 National Oceanic and Atmospheric Administration (NOAA) publication *Tropical Cyclones of the North Atlantic Ocean, 1871–1998*, Historical Climatology Series 6-2; U.S. Weather Bureau reports of Climatological Data (for Florida, 1897–1965); and *Monthly Weather Review.*

It should be noted that this book deals primarily with the characteristics of Florida hurricanes and tropical storms and some eyewitness accounts. Amounts of precipitation associated with Florida hurricanes are noted but not discussed because large amounts of rainfall also frequently result from other systems, such as tropical depressions or nontropical systems. However, we should point out that precipitation from a hurricane or tropical storm can be heavy and can cause major damage and flooding. Tropical depressions (TD) can also cause heavy flooding problems and damage. Tropical waves and depressions are not named, but depressions are numbered TD1, TD2, and so on. Some of the direct quotes we use make reference to the earlier terms *Great Hurricane* and *Major Hurricane*. The glossary and tables explain the terms formerly used and the Saffir/Simpson Scale now in use to categorize hurricanes.

We are especially thankful to the reviewers of the original manuscript, who pointed out several deficiencies and errors and provided important suggestions leading to improved accuracy. We are especially thankful to friends, colleagues, assistants, and organizations, without whose help we could not have developed the work. Specifically, we thank the following people for help in preparing the first edition: Bill Mahan, who encouraged us; Annette Bernard, Ann Bergonzoni, Derrick Doehring, Rosary Pedreira, Arnold Samreth, and Huan Feng for manuscript preparation; Henry (Hank) Brandli for graciously providing us with satellite images of Florida hurricanes; Anita Bromberg and John

Reposa, who assisted in preparation of the plates showing hurricane tracks; Victoria (Tori) Smith and Jeanette C. Sparks of the Florida Tech Evans Library for searching historical documents; Florida Sea Grant College, which provided financial assistance; Jay Humphreys, who read the manuscript and provided suggestions for improvement; the *News/Sun Sentinel* of Ft. Lauderdale and the *Miami Herald* for use of their photographs; Ruth Warner for kindly providing her grandmother's account of the 1926 Miami hurricane; Lois Stephens for allowing us to use her personal account of Hurricane Andrew, titled "On Sabbatical with Hurricane Andrew"; and the National Hurricane Center for providing photographs.

In preparing all editions, we are especially thankful to the office of the National Weather Service in Melbourne for providing Doppler radar images and other information. The following people were very helpful: Hank Brandli, who provided several images for this book; Mike Witiw, formerly of Florida Tech, who also provided satellite images; Vern Miller, Tom Needham, and Tracy Wilcox of the *Panama City News Herald,* who kindly supplied photographs of hurricane damage from Opal, Allison, and Erin; Nina Williams, also of Panama City, who sent pictures and articles about Opal; Susan Hurd, Kathleen Lisa, and Kuei-Tin (Katy) Hsu for assistance with word processing and software; Larry Floyd for photographs of Hurricane Andrew damage; Richard Clark, who provided historical photographs of the 1926 Miami hurricane; and Susan Grantham of Florida Sea Grant College, who patiently worked with us on all aspects of the book.

Finally, in the present revised edition, we are very grateful to Robert Gribbroek of Florida Tech's University Publications for assistance in file conversions and to Dr. Anne Steinemann for final proofreading.

I

Introduction

A hurricane is an extremely violent whirling and spiraling tropical cyclone, shaped somewhat like a funnel, that frequently originates in tropical regions of the North Atlantic Ocean, Caribbean Sea, Gulf of Mexico, Western Pacific Ocean, Eastern Pacific Ocean, South Pacific, China Sea, and Indian Ocean. The Cape Verde Islands off the western coast of Africa are often the breeding grounds of some of the most powerful hurricanes to strike the United States.

The term *cyclone*, used by weathermen and meteorologists, refers to an area of low pressure in which winds move around the pressure center and are usually attended by foul weather and strong wind speeds. A tropical cyclone is a large-scale, warm-core, low-pressure storm that develops not along a front but over tropical or subtropical waters and that has a definite organized circulation.

Tropical cyclones are called typhoons in the Western North Pacific Ocean and South Pacific Ocean; hurricanes in the Eastern North Pacific and Atlantic Basin; *baguios* in the South China Sea; cyclones in the Indian Ocean; and willy-willies in Australia.

The size of a typical tropical cyclone can vary considerably depending on the extent of the wind fields and rain fields. In a relatively large hurricane, such as the Florida hurricane of September 1947, hurricane winds can extend 100 miles from the center (the distance from Palm Beach to Melbourne). However, Hurricane Andrew in August 1992—the most destructive hurricane ever to strike Florida or the U.S. mainland—had its maximum winds with a radius of only about 12.5 miles.

For a storm to be officially classified as a hurricane, wind speed in a tropical cyclone must be 74 miles per hour or greater. The direction of rotation of wind in a tropical cyclone is counterclockwise in the Northern Hemisphere and clockwise in the Southern Hemisphere. The average hurricane's center, referred to as the eye, is about 20 miles in diameter. The eye is surrounded by hurricane force winds and is known as the wall cloud or eye wall. Outside the wall cloud, or area of maximum winds, winds decrease fairly rapidly to tropical storm force or less.

Within the hurricane, barometric pressure is 1–3 inches of mercury below the standard atmospheric pressure at sea level, which is 29.92 inches.

The North Atlantic hurricane season occurs during the months of June through November, with September generally having the greatest number of storms. The total number of hurricanes or tropical storms shows great variation from year to year. In fact, certain past multi-decadal periods have had significantly greater numbers of hurricanes than others. This is supported by the work of William M. Gray (1990), who reported that the period from the late 1940s through the late 1960s had a much larger number of hurricanes—that is, it had a strong cycle—than did the 1970s and 1980s, except for Gilbert in 1988 in the Caribbean and Hugo in 1989 in the United States (1988 and 1989 were weak cycle years). The year of Hurricane Andrew, 1992, was also a weak cycle year. The average year involves about nine named storms with six of these becoming hurricanes. Possibly two of the hurricanes will be intense, meaning Category 3, 4, or 5 on the Saffir/Simpson Scale (table 1).

In a passage from his 1990 article "Strong Association Between West African Rainfall and U.S. Landfall of Intense Hurricanes," Gray notes: "Seasonal and multi-decadal variations of intense hurricane activity are closely linked to seasonal and multi-decadal variations of summer rainfall amounts in the Western Sahel region of West Africa. In general, the annual frequency of intense Atlantic hurricanes was appreciably greater from 1947 to 1969, when plentiful amounts of rainfall occurred in West Africa, than during the years between 1970 and 1987, when drought conditions prevailed." Dr. Gray also includes other parameters in the study.

The average forward movement of a hurricane approaching the Florida coastline is 6–15 mph. The direction of movement relative to the coastline has a large bearing on added destructive forces, with the perpendicular landfall being the most dangerous situation. This is because the wind field in a hurricane is typically asymmetric, the strongest wind generally being within the right-front quadrant of the storm as viewed in the direction of movement and with the forward speed added to the wind speed. The right-front quadrant is the side of the wind field that produces the strongest storm surge, which in most cases is the most destructive part of the hurricane.

Goldenberg et al. (2001), in their paper in *Science* magazine, attribute the recent increase in hurricane activity in the Atlantic basin generally to simultaneous increases in North Atlantic sea-surface temperatures and changes in the speed of winds at different altitudes, which is called vertical wind shear.

A storm surge, also called a hurricane surge, is the abnormal rise in sea level accompanying a tropical cyclone. The height of the storm surge is the difference between the observed level of the sea surface and its level in the absence of the storm. The storm surge is estimated by subtracting the normal or astronomical tide from the observed or estimated storm tide. Surge heights vary considerably and result from a combination of direct winds and atmospheric pressure. Additional factors are water transport by waves, swells, rainfall, and shoreline configuration; bottom topography; and tide height at the time the storm hits the coast. As an example of an extreme storm surge, Hurricane Donna, which struck the Florida Keys in 1960, caused a surge of an estimated 12 to 14 feet, which was significant considering that there are few structures and little terrain that high in the Keys. More catastrophic was the 24.4-foot surge resulting from Hurricane Camille, which struck the Mississippi coastline in 1969. The potentially devastating effects of the storm surge are further illustrated if one considers that a cubic yard of seawater weighs nearly three-fourths of a ton, which pretty well guarantees destruction of anything in its path.

The storm surge has a tendency to dissipate the farther inland it goes, particularly if the land rises in elevation. However, winds and flooding still remain problems. High winds, the storm surge, battering waves, and high tide make a hurricane a potential killer with accompanying devastation and huge losses to property. In addition, tornadoes can be spawned by hurricanes, adding to the overall threat.

Torrential rainfall, which can also occur in a hurricane, adds to the life-threatening and major damaging effects by causing floods and flash floods. For example, the aftermath of Hurricane Agnes—a relatively weak Florida hurricane but well known as one of the costliest hurricanes in the Mid-Atlantic states—resulted in severe inland flooding from torrential rainfall when it merged with another weather system in mountainous areas. In this case the hurricane surge at landfall played only a small part in the total destruction that resulted.

High winds alone can lead to a barrage of flying debris, including tree limbs and branches, signs and signposts, roofing (even entire roofs in major storms), and metal siding, all of which can move through the air like missiles.

Except when crossing completely flat, wet areas, such as in extreme south Florida, hurricanes usually weaken rapidly as they move inland. Hurricane Andrew actually intensified slightly as it passed over the swampy area of extreme south Florida. However, the remnants of a hurricane can bring 6 to 12 inches of rain or more to an area as the storm passes. Should a weakened hurricane on land return to the sea, it could regain strength.

It is clear, then, that entire communities, including residential and business buildings, can be wiped out by a hurricane.

Because of the difficulty in relating the different and varying factors or characteristics of a hurricane to the destruction, the Saffir/Simpson Scale was conceived in 1972 and introduced to the public in 1975. This scale, named for Herbert Saffir and Robert Simpson, has been used for over 20 years to estimate the relative damage potential of a hurricane due to wind and storm surge. The Saffir/Simpson Scale classifies hurricanes into Categories 1, 2, 3, 4, and 5, depending upon the barometric pressure, wind speed, and storm surge and destruction (table 1). A Category 1 hurricane, for example, would inflict minimal damage, primarily to shrubbery, trees, foliage, unanchored structures, mobile homes, small craft, and low-lying areas that could become flooded. A Category 4 or 5 hurricane would cause catastrophic damage such as blown down trees, power lines, and poles; overturned vehicles; torn down or blown away buildings; complete destruction of mobile or manufactured homes and of entire mobile home parks; and massive flooding.

After Hurricane Andrew, the Fujita Tornado Scale was used to assess damage. Dr. Theodore Fujita was an expert on tornadoes and severe weather. This scale of F0 to F5 indicates winds from 40 mph to over 260 mph.[1] Evidence showed that there was a possibility of F3 and F4 tornado activity in the wall cloud of Andrew.

The practical usefulness of the Saffir/Simpson Scale is that it relates properties of the hurricane to previously observed damage. Until the Saffir/Simpson Scale was developed, hurricanes were referred to as Great Hurricanes, Severe Hurricanes, or Minor, Minimal, Major, or Extreme Hurricanes (table 2); these terms are no longer used but crop up in historical material. Tropical storms are named but are not assigned a Saffir/Simpson category number.

Note

1. The Fugita tornado scale is as follows:

F0 = 40–72 mph

F1 = 73–112 mph

F2 = 113–157 mph

F3 = 158–206 mph

F4 = 207–260 mph

F5 = >260 mph.

2

Florida's Hurricane History

Florida is considered synonymous with sunshine and is frequently called the Sunshine State, but mention of the state also brings to mind summer or fall tropical storms and hurricanes. These storms move in a westerly to northwesterly direction through the Caribbean and Atlantic toward Florida's east coast and generally northward in the Gulf of Mexico. From 1493 to 1870, the Caribbean area and Florida experienced nearly 400 hurricanes, as reported by E. B. Garriott in 1900 in his classic study *West Indian Hurricanes*. Many Spanish galleons loaded with gold, silver, and other treasure must have met a swift and untimely demise at the hand of a hurricane or tropical storm. As a result, treasure hunting is an active and frequently profitable business today in Florida.

From 1871 through 2001, over 1,000 tropical cyclones have occurred in the North Atlantic, Caribbean Sea, and Gulf of Mexico. Of this total, about 200 have reached Florida, with 75 of these known to have had hurricane force winds (wind speed of 74 mph or greater) and 83 known to have had winds of tropical storm force (39–73 mph).

During the 15 years from 1871 to 1885, there were 31 tropical cyclones of unknown intensity (shown by solid lines on tracking plates 1 and 2). Historical data indicate that some of these were hurricanes. Because these hurricanes have not been officially documented, they are listed as a combined total number of storms for the purposes of an overall count of Florida hurricanes (table 3).

In the last 130 years, there have been as many as 21 hurricanes and tropical storms during a single year (in 1933), and there have been 33 years during which no tropical cyclones made a Florida landfall or their centers passed immediately offshore of the coastline (Fernandina Beach to Key West to Pensacola). It should be emphasized that most data gathered before 1900 are sketchy, though some accounts are detailed. Most data obtained after World War II are reliable.

While early records are fragmentary and incomplete, the following do permit a discussion of the more formidable Florida hurricanes. For convenience and to provide readable hurricane tracks, our discussion examines hurricanes occurring within 10-year periods. When possible the Saffir/Simpson Scale (table 1) is applied to describe the hurricane category for both past hurricanes (before the scale was developed) and recent hurricanes.

1871–1900

Starting in 1871, only a few years after the Civil War, tropical cyclone data became part of the historical inventory of the U.S. Signal Service and later the U.S. Department of Agriculture Weather Bureau, which collected, archived, and published these data. Relying on early works such as *West Indian Hurricanes* (Garriott, 1900), annual tropical cyclone tracks for the years 1871–1990 were later published in the NOAA Historical Climatology Series 6-2, *Tropical Cyclones of the North Atlantic Ocean, 1871–1998* (NOAA, 1999). The yearly tracks were extracted from that NOAA publication and are presented here by 10-year periods.

Looking at the first 10 years of tropical cyclone tracks (tracking plate 1), the most striking feature is that only four tropical cyclones entered Florida's coast from the east, southeast, Atlantic, or Caribbean. In contrast, 17 tropical cyclones entered the west coast and Panhandle region from the southwest, the northwestern Caribbean, and Gulf of Mexico. The periods 1881–90 and 1891–1900 (tracking plates 2 and 3) show essentially the same pattern, except that the concentration of northeasterly tracks shifts farther to the south. We shall see from an examination of the other plates that this pattern changed after the turn of the century. Principally, all of the storms that entered the west coast of Florida came from the northwestern Caribbean or the southern portion of the Gulf of Mexico.

There are some contradictory events reported during these early years that merit discussion. They pertain to the hurricanes of 1876, 1880, and 1885. In an interview published on June 4, 1978, in the newspaper *Florida Today,* then National Hurricane Center director Dr. Neil Frank said: "In [August] 1871 the center of a hurricane slammed into Central Florida near Cocoa Beach. . . . In [September–October] 1873 a major hurricane exited Florida near Melbourne. . . . In [August–September] 1880 another major hurricane battered the coast south of Cocoa Beach."

The 1880 hurricane that "battered the coast south of Cocoa Beach" was classified in Norton's *Florida Hurricanes* (1949) as a Great Hurricane. According to his notes, it affected the Palm Beach–Lake Okeechobee section of Florida; nothing is said about Cocoa Beach. But Dunn and Miller in *Atlantic Hurricanes* (1964) said that the hurricane affected Vero Beach. However, the 1880 track as extracted from NOAA's Historical Climatology Series 6-2 (NOAA, 1999) shows a hurricane entering the east coast near Cocoa Beach. The area affected by this hurricane could not have been the Palm Beach–Lake Okeechobee section if the hurricane entered Florida on the east coast from the east-southeast near Cocoa Beach. If, on the other hand, Norton is correct in his finding, then the 1880 hurricane track reported by NOAA has to be in error—the track would be a considerable distance south of Cocoa Beach. This contention is amply supported by the hurricane track of August 26–31, 1880, reported by Garriott (1900) and by the August 1880 track Tannehill published in *Hurricanes: Their Nature and History* (1938).

In reference to the August 1885 hurricane, the track published by NOAA (1999) along the east coast may also be in error in that it is at least 20 miles offshore. As described in B. Rabac's *The City of Cocoa Beach* (1986): "The hurricane that hit in 1885 discouraged further settlement. The storm pushed the ocean waves over the barrier island (elevation 10 feet), flooding out the homesteaders. The beach near the Canaveral Light House was severely eroded, prompting President Cleveland and the Congress to allot money for an effort to move the tower one mile west."

The fact that President Cleveland was in office from 1885 to 1888 provides further support that this was the year of occurrence. It is certainly possible that the 1885 northerly tropical cyclone track shown over the ocean along the Florida east coast on the NOAA track chart (NOAA, 1999) was slightly displaced from the correct position and that the eye of the hurricane actually passed Cocoa Beach. A report by Sugg,

Pardue, and Carrodus (1971) shows the 1885 track passing the central east coast.

The final controversy concerns the hurricane of 1876. Historical information from Dr. G. W. Holmes in a letter to a friend that year indicates that the eye of a terrible hurricane passed over Eau Gallie (now part of Melbourne) on the Indian River Lagoon on a northerly course one early morning in 1876 (no date or month was given). Holmes wrote: "The wind came from the east at over a hundred miles an hour until about 3:30 A.M.. The vortex [the eye] came on us for about four hours, during which not a leaf stirred. We began to look for our boats when all at once with a tremendous roar the wind came from the west, with equal violence [to that] in the early part of the night."

The letter implies that the hurricane traveled north along the Indian River Lagoon or beaches. NOAA (1999) shows a northerly hurricane track for the year 1876, about 30–40 miles east of the coast, passing Cape Canaveral during September 12–19, 1876. The 1876 hurricane could easily be off by 30 miles, which would bring the eye over Melbourne and make valid the effect Holmes describes. In October 12–22, another hurricane exited near West Palm Beach from the west. However, until NOAA officially modifies hurricane tracks for 1876, 1880, and 1885, they have to be accepted as given from NOAA's track book and shown in tracking plates 1 and 2.

Beginning in 1886, tropical storm and hurricane tracks were published separately. We presented them in dashed and solid lines with the year circled at the beginning of each track (tracking plates 2–14). A solid line prior to 1886 indicates either a tropical storm or hurricane. From 1886 onward, a solid line crossing the coast indicates a hurricane, and a dashed line indicates a tropical storm. Starting with the year 1899, tracks became more detailed and categories were used to describe the relative magnitude of hurricanes.

We conclude this section with information about two hurricanes that entered Florida in 1898 and 1899.

Hurricane of October 2–3, 1898, Fernandina Beach

An official monthly report (U.S. Weather Bureau, October 1898) included this account of the 1898 hurricane: "The damage to Fernandina and vicinity was very great. It is conservatively estimated at $500,000. Nothing escaped damage and a great deal was absolutely destroyed. Giant oaks were snapped off at the base, houses blown down, and vessels swept inland by an irresistible in-rush of water. The wind signal display man Major W.B.C. Duryee, who has resided in Fernandina more than thirty years, states that no previous storm was so severe."

Professor F. H. Bigelow (1898) provided this rather elegant description of a hurricane, published in the *Yearbook of the Department of Agriculture*.

> The physical features of hurricanes are well understood. The approach of a hurricane is usually indicated by a long swell on the ocean, propagated to great distances and forewarning the observer by two or three days. A faint rise in the barometer occurs before the gradual fall, which becomes very pronounced at the center; fine wisps of cirrus clouds are seen, which surround the center to a distance of 200 miles: the air is calm and sultry, but this is gradually supplanted by a gentle breeze, and later the wind increases to a gale, the clouds become matted, the sea rough, rain falls, and the winds are gusty and dangerous as the vortex core comes on. Here is the indescribable tempest, dealing destruction, impressing the imagination with its wild exhibition of the forces of nature, the flashes of lightning, the torrents of rain, the cooler air, all the elements in an uproar, which indicate the close approach of the center. In the midst of this turmoil there is a sudden pause, the winds almost cease, the sky clears, the waves, however, rage in the great turbulence. This is the eye of the storm, the core of the vortex, and it is, perhaps, 20 miles in diameter, or one-thirtieth of the whole hurricane. The respite is brief and is soon followed by the abrupt renewal of the violent wind and rain, but now coming from the opposite direction, and the storm passes off with the features following each other in the reverse order. There is probably no feature of nature more interesting to study than a hurricane, though feelings of the observer may sometimes be diverted by thoughts of personal safety!

Hurricane of August 1, 1899, Carrabelle

The U.S. Weather Bureau's 1899 annual report gave details about this hurricane: "After reaching the coast and maintaining very high velocities from the northeast backing to the North and West for 10 hours, the storm gradually abated leaving the town of Carrabelle a wreck. The results to shipping were disastrous, 14 barks (transport sailboats) and 40 vessels under 20 tons having been wrecked. The loss of life was amazingly small, the total being only six. The property loss, including vessels and cargo will amount to $500,000."

1901–1930

This 30-year period had less tropical storm and hurricane activity than either the preceding or the following 30 years. From 1901 to 1930, Florida saw a combined total of 42 tropical storms and hurricanes, compared to 63 during the preceding 30 years, 1871–1900, and 51 for 1931–60. Storms during the first three decades of the twentieth century came primarily from the southwest.

U.S. Weather Bureau records (1901–30) in table 3 show that there were 20 hurricanes and 20 tropical storms during this period; those classified as hurricanes are named and listed in table 4. With the availability of more factual data published in the Climatological Data bulletins since 1897, information now becomes more accurate and detailed, consisting of actual reports for those years.

Looking at the first 10-year segment (1901–10), the Great Hurricane of October 1910 did a loop north of the western tip of Cuba (Norton, 1949), passed through Key West, and entered the coast near Fort Myers, where a low pressure of 28.20 inches of mercury was reported. This was probably one of the most destructive hurricanes to hit Florida, a Category 3 storm. At Key West there was a 15-foot storm tide, and Sand Key reported 125 mph winds. The U.S. Army and Marine Hospital Docks were swept away at Key West, but little other narrative information is available on the storm except that it made landfall near Cape Romano.

Although it is touted in stories and movies as a typical hurricane setting, Key West is not unduly hurricane-prone. The last encounter was in September 1998, Hurricane Georges; the previous one was Floyd in 1987. Before Floyd, it had been 21 years, all the way back to Hurricane Inez in 1966, since a hurricane had struck the Keys. In 1965 Hurricane Betsy sideswiped the "Conch Capital," as did Isbell in 1964. These storms followed a 14-year lull during which the Keys were untouched by hurricanes. In 1950, Easy struck the Keys, bringing to an end the area's 31 years of calm going back to 1919. From 1871 to 2001, Key West was hit by 15 tropical cyclones, or about 10 percent of the storms discussed here.

Other hurricanes during the 1901–10 period were those of September 1906, which practically destroyed Pensacola, and of 1909. For these two storms there is good documentation that is worth further discussion.

Hurricane of September 19–29, 1906, Mobile-Pensacola Area

According to the 1906 U.S. Weather Bureau report, this was a major storm: "This was the most terrific storm in the history of Pensacola, or since the Village of Pensacola on Santa Rosa Island was swept away 170 years ago. . . . During the height of the storm, the water rose 8 ½ feet above normal high water mark, being the highest known. The entire water front property was inundated; train service in and out of the city was completely paralyzed. . . . Muskogee Wharf, belonging to the L&N Railroad Co., was broken in two in the middle, and the tracks on either side of the Main Creek were washed away [including thirty-eight coal cars]. . . . The greatest havoc was wrought along east Main Street, the south side of which has been completely washed away. The total damage from this hurricane will be three to four million dollars [equivalent to $80–100 million in 1990]."

This hurricane made landfall in Alabama but affected Pensacola; because of this storm, 164 people lost their lives. Other storm notes by the U.S. Weather Bureau for the hurricane of September 1906 are from three other counties. From St. Andrews, Washington County: "On the 26th, a tidal wave swept this place; the water was higher than any time during the past 19 years, and every wharf in St. Andrews was completely destroyed." From Apalachicola, Franklin County: "On the 27th, the wind blew a gale from the southeast, and on the 28th, it increased to a hurricane velocity. The amount of rainfall was 10.12 inches." And from Galt, Santa Rosa County: "The storm of the 26–28th was the worst ever known in this section; on the 26th, the tide rose 14 feet. Two lives were lost here" (U.S. Weather Bureau, 1906).

Hurricane of October 6–13, 1909, Sand Key

Tannehill (1938) provides the following discussion of the October 1909 hurricane that struck Sand Key and resulted in 15 deaths:

> The hurricane of October 1909 was one of exceptional intensity. It re-curved over the extreme southern tip of Florida, at which time it had attained tremendous force. The Weather Bureau had a station at Sand Key, Florida which was abandoned at 8:30 A.M., and supplies and instruments were carried to the lighthouse. The wind was then 75 miles an hour; shortly thereafter, the anemometer cups were carried away and the wind was estimated at 100 miles an hour. All the trees were blown down and at 9:35 A.M. heavy seas swept over the island. At 10:30 A.M., the Weather Bureau building went over and was swept out to sea. The lowest barometer reading was 28.36 inches. At Key West the barometer fell to 28.50 inches and the extreme wind velocity was 94 miles. Property damage there amounted to $1,000,000 [equivalent to $20 million in 1990]. About four hundred buildings collapsed.

During the second 10-year segment (1911–20), there were four hurricanes, including one Great Hurricane that deserves mention. Three of these, all with winds over 100 mph, affected the Pensacola area again, like the hurricane of September 1906.

Hurricane of July 1916, Mobile-Pensacola Area

The U.S. Weather Bureau (July 1916) reported that at 1:00 P.M., "a 92 mile per hour gale occurred with severe puffs from the southeast. The duration of the gale was extraordinary, and the total damage to the crops and the property will easily total $1,000,000 [equivalent to $20 million in 1990] for the section." This hurricane made landfall in Mississippi, where four lives were lost.

Hurricane of October 1916, Pensacola

The barometric pressure in this storm was 28.76 inches at Pensacola. "The wind instrument tower at the Weather Bureau Office blew down at 10:14 A.M., after registering an extreme rate of 120 mph at 10:13 A.M. Oak trees that withstood the July storm were uprooted; about 200 trees throughout the city were blown down" (U.S. Weather Bureau, October 1916).

Hurricane of November 1916, Florida Keys

This system started in the Caribbean and moved northwest through the Yucatan Channel and into the Keys on November 15. Minimal damage resulted from this Category 1 storm.

Hurricane of September 1917, Pensacola-Valparaiso Area

"This was a very severe storm, doing much damage on the coast and to crops. The lowest barometer reading, 28.51 inches, was a record for the Pensacola Station. The highest wind velocity during the storm was 103 miles an hour with an extreme rate of 125 miles an hour from the southeast" (U.S. Weather Bureau, September 1917).

The Great Hurricane of September 1919, Key West

The following report on the Great Hurricane of September 1919 is quoted from NOAA (1999) but came originally from U.S. Weather Bureau records for September 1919: "The storm that passed over Key West on September 9 and 10 was, without question, the most violent of any recorded at this station. Property loss is estimated at 2 million [equivalent to $40 million in 1990]. In the terrific gusts that prevailed during the height of the storm, staunch brick structures had walls blown out, and large vessels which had been firmly secured, were torn from their moorings and blown on the banks."

The lowest barometric pressure was 27.37 inches of mercury at the Dry Tortugas. At Key West, where winds were 110 mph, 300 lives were lost. According to a recent NOAA report by Hebert, Jarrell, and Mayfield (1995), this storm ranked third among the most intense hurricanes to strike the United States this century until Hurricane Andrew took over that ranking in August 1992.

During the last ten years of the period from 1901 to 1930, there were six interesting hurricanes, including two Great Hurricanes that could be considered equivalent to Category 4 hurricanes, according to the Saffir/Simpson Scale. Some descriptions of these storms follow.

Hurricane of October 20, 1921, Tarpon Springs

"Great damage resulted at Tampa and adjacent sections from the combined effects of high winds and storm tides. The tide at Tampa was 10.5 feet, the highest since 1848. Eggmond and Sanibel Island were practically covered by water" (U.S. Weather Bureau, October 1921). Barometric pressure was 28.11 inches at Tarpon Springs, and winds were more than 100 mph.

Only one hurricane and one tropical storm were recorded for Florida in 1925. The storm that came ashore near Tampa on November 30 was significant from a statistical standpoint as it was the latest date on which any storm had hit the United States during hurricane season.

Hurricane of July 26–28, 1926, Indian River

"The Center was near Palm Beach on the morning of the 27th, then moved north-northwestward. The high winds and seas swept before them boats, docks, boat houses and other marine property on the ocean front as well as that on the Indian River Lagoon. Trees were uprooted, including citrus trees; houses were unroofed or otherwise damaged. The observer at Merritt Island remarks that there was a tremendous wave (this on the Indian River Lagoon) and with the high wind all boats, docks, and other property from the river front were swept ashore" (U.S. Weather Bureau, July 1926).

The Great Miami Hurricane of September 11–27, 1926

"From the viewpoint of property loss, low barometric pressure, and maximum wind velocities at Miami, the hurricane of September, 1926, stands unchallenged in the meteorological records of the Weather Bureau, save only in respect to the loss of life at Galveston during the hurricane of 1900. The storm waters of the Atlantic united with the waters of Biscayne Bay and swept westward into the City of Miami. . . . This was the most severe storm that ever visited this city. The extreme velocity was registered at 7:26 A.M. The average velocity for the 20th was 76.2 miles an hour. Never before have hurricane winds been recorded for so long a time and never has the wind maintained a velocity of 100 miles for more than a hour" (U.S. Weather Bureau, September 1926; see figs. 1.A–C). Winds and barometric pressure of this storm were 138 mph and 27.61 inches of mercury, respectively. Richard Clark kindly provided historical photographs of this storm (figs. 1.D–I).

The following excerpts are from copies of letters kindly donated by Mrs. Ruth Warner of Barefoot Bay, Florida, documenting the experience of her grandmother, Mrs. Lucia Lawrence, in the 1926 Miami hurricane. Mrs. Lawrence wrote in September and on October 2, 1926:

> The weather bureau broadcasted that a hurricane of great intensity was headed for the east coast, but that around Jupiter would be the center of the storm, but Miami got it.
>
> About midnight, the wind was blowing a gale and the electric lights went out; everything in darkness.
>
> When we got candles lighted, [we] found the water pouring through the ceilings on the rear half of the house so we knew the roofing was off.
>
> With daylight Saturday came a lull in the wind for about 45 minutes. A good many (people) didn't know it was the center of the storm and so were fooled. Mrs. Moran (a friend at whose house they were staying) says the worst is yet to come but it will come from another direction. Sure enough the puffs soon began coming, but from the southeast. Before that it was from the north east.
>
> We all huddled in the dining room and kitchen until it was over, expecting every moment to feel and see the house going to pieces, at least, the front caving in as it rocked and swayed as the gusts struck.
>
> We nailed the doors, watched the screens and awnings go. Said we had done all we could do and left the rest with God.
>
> The fury of the storm was terrible. It made such a peculiar

muffled roaring sound in the air above. There are about 18,000 homes, either completely demolished or roofs torn off. About 5,000 injured and a good many more dead than the papers give, I believe. Probably a good many from the boats will never be found.

It's some mess to have all ones bedding blankets, clothing and bureau contents soaked at the same time.

Hurricane of August 7–8, 1928, Indian River Lagoon

"Damage to property was heaviest from South Brevard to St. Lucie Counties. . . . Substantial houses were unroofed and frail ones were razed. Highways were flooded and badly washed. Many bridges were undermined requiring replacement. Many citrus trees were uprooted, the loss of fruit estimated at 1,000,000 boxes. Large oaks, sentinels of a century, were uprooted" (U.S. Weather Bureau, 1928).

The Deadly Great Lake Okeechobee Hurricane of September 6–20, 1928

This Category 4 storm tracked across Lake Okeechobee's northern shore, causing the shallow waters to reach heights of more than 15 feet. The surge was forced southward, causing terrible flooding in the low-lands at the lake's south end, a region farmed primarily by migrant workers. Thousands of migrant farmers died as water rushed over the area. After the storm, the Red Cross counted 1,836 dead, but still more bodies and skeletons were discovered in later years. The barometric pressure was measured at 27.43 inches. To prevent future similar disasters, dikes were built around the lake by the U.S. Army Corps of Engineers.

The 1928 storm caused $25 million in damage (equivalent to $300 million in 1990 dollars; figs. 2.A–B). Hebert and colleagues (1995) report that this hurricane ranked second among the deadliest hurricanes to strike the United States and was ranked fourth among the most intense hurricanes to strike the nation. Today this storm falls to fifth place in intensity, after Hurricane Andrew, which struck south Florida in August 1992 with a low barometric pressure of 27.23 inches.

Hurricane of September 28, 1929, Key Largo

Tannehill (1938) provides the following account of this hurricane striking the Keys: "The center passed over Key Largo on the 28th, barometer about 28 inches and wind estimated at 150 miles an hour. There was a ten-minute lull as the center passed. At Long Key the barometer was 28.18 inches. At the Everglades, the wind was estimated at 100 miles an hour, barometer 28.95 inches. The storm reached Panama City on the 30th, barometer 28.80 inches. Although there was enormous damage at Nassau in the Bahamas and many lives were lost there, its course in Florida was such that damage probably did not exceed $500,000 [$6 million in 1990 dollars] and only three lives were lost. The population had been thoroughly warned by the Weather Bureau and there had been ample time for all possible precautions."

1931–1960

As earlier noted, the 30-year period from 1931 to 1960 had more storm activity than did the preceding 30 years—51 total storms compared to 42. There were 22 hurricanes, almost the same as the number reported for the previous period. However, tropical storms numbered 29 compared to 20 for the previous 30 years, which accounts for the high number of total storms.

The temporal distribution of hurricanes from 1931 to 1960 is interesting. While there were few hurricanes in 1931–40 (six) and 1951–60 (three), there were 12 hurricanes for the 10-year period 1941–50 alone. This made the 1941–50 segment the most destructive and costliest period to that date, in terms of equivalent dollar value, since records had been kept for the state. Yet ten years later in 1960, one single hurricane, the Category 4 Donna, was even more costly and destructive than all the storms in the 10 years from 1941 to 1950 (Hebert et al., 1995).

Looking at the six hurricanes of first decade (1931–40), two were Category 3 storms and one in 1935 was a Category 5 hurricane, one of only two Category 5 hurricanes ever to hit the U.S. coast with that intensity. The other was Hurricane Camille, which struck Mississippi in 1969. Hurricane Allen, which struck Texas in 1980, reached Category

5 intensity three times during its path but weakened to Category 3 at landfall (Hebert et al., 1995).

The Major Hurricane of September 1933, Jupiter

In July and September 1933, two hurricanes entered the east coast of Florida within a short distance of each other. The second of these, which occurred on Labor Day, deserves review.

"There was much property damage on the east coast from Vero Beach to Palm Beach; a few houses were totally demolished, quite a number blown off their blocks. More than the equivalent of 4 million boxes of citrus were blown from the trees statewide. The property loss in Indian River, St. Lucie, and Palm Beach Counties probably was about 2 million dollars [$25 million in 1990]" (U.S. Weather Bureau, September 1933). An elderly citizen from Fort Pierce recalled that the 1933 storm was the most devastating in the history of the area (Yanaros, pers. comm., 1986).

In 1935 two hurricanes visited southern Florida. The first was the Great Labor Day Hurricane of September 1935, and the other was the storm called the Yankee Hurricane (October 30–November 8) because it came in from a northeasterly direction and struck the extreme south Florida coast and the west coast.

The Great Labor Day Hurricane of 1935, Category 5

The Great Labor Day Hurricane was the most violent in the history of Florida, the United States, and the Atlantic basin. It was the only Category 5 storm ever to strike Florida; its central barometric pressure of 26.35 inches of mercury was the lowest ever recorded at that time in the Northern Hemisphere. (As of 1988, Hurricane Gilbert, which did not affect Florida, has held the record for the lowest barometric pressure in the Northern Hemisphere, 26.22 inches).

The following excerpt about the 1935 storm is from Norton's *Florida Hurricanes* (1949): "No anemometer reading of the wind was obtained, but the gradient formula gives 200–250 mph and the engineer's estimate by stress formula is in substantial agreement . . . the path of destruction was less than 40 miles in width. More than 400 people were killed, most by drowning. The tracks of the Flagler Railroad were washed from the Long Key viaduct at an elevation of 30 feet above mean low water. A survey by the U.S. Engineers some time after the storm indicated that the tide level never reached the rails there, but the hurricane surge superimposed on the tide probably assisted in carrying the tracks away." (The maximum storm surge with Hurricane Camille was 24.2 feet.)

Tannehill (1938) described a tragic event of the 1935 storm: "A rescue train that was sent to remove World War I veterans and residents from the Florida Keys, on September 2, 1935, was swept from the tracks by the hurricane and the storm wave" (fig. 3.A–D).

The following 10-year period, 1941–1950, was the most devastating decade in Florida's history since records had been kept. Out of 12 hurricanes, 11 struck between 1944 and 1950. In this relatively short period a Category 4 storm reached Florida in 1947 and there were six Category 3 hurricanes, one each in 1944, 1945, 1948, and 1949 and two in 1950; a Category 1 storm struck Fort Myers on the west coast in 1946.

The following description of the 1944 storm is from the U.S. Weather Bureau report for October 1944:

> Dangerous winds extended fully 200 miles to the right or east of the center, about 100 miles to the left or west, thus affecting the entire peninsula of Florida. (Even at Dry Tortugas, barometric pressure was 28.02 inches of mercury.) Winds of hurricane force velocity surrounded the central core, with gusts up to 100 mph at Tampa and Orlando. Tides were high from Sarasota southward on the Gulf and from Melbourne northward on the Atlantic. Naples, and Jacksonville Beach reported 12-foot tides. Citrus loss was over 21 million boxes (average harvest was 80 million). Throughout the state there was damage to telephone, telegraph and power lines, trees, roofs, chimneys, signs, and radio towers. Of the interior cities, Orlando seems to have suffered the most damage, being estimated at over one million dollars.

The next hurricane of importance entered the coast in September 1945 at Homestead, curving northward right up through the center of Florida. Wind speed decreased during this course, but the storm maintained itself as one with minimal hurricane force. It remained over land to exit near Jacksonville Beach. The tragic event in this storm was the destruction at Richmond, Florida, of the three Navy blimp hangars that were used as evacuation shelters for 25 Navy blimps, 183 military planes, 153 civilian planes, and 150 automobiles. The three great hangars were torn to pieces at the height of the storm and then caught fire and burned with all their contents; the total loss was estimated at $35 million (U.S. Weather Bureau, September 1945).

Then came the Category 4 hurricane of September 17, 1947, clocking the highest recorded wind speed in Florida's history. A one-minute maximum wind speed of 155 mph was recorded by a reliable instrument at the Hillsboro (Pompano Beach) light station. Not until Hurricane Andrew in 1992 were higher wind speeds recorded. The following account describes this exceptionally strong hurricane (U.S. Weather Bureau, September 1947): "Hurricane force winds were experienced along the Florida East Coast from about Cape Canaveral to Carysfort Reef Light (south of Miami), a distance of about 240 miles, while winds of 100 mph, or over, were felt from the northern portion of Miami to well north of Palm Beach, or about 70 miles. This classifies this hurricane as one of the great storms of recent years."

This September 1947 storm had a barometric pressure of 27.97 inches of mercury at Hillsboro, with tides at Clewiston and Moore Haven of 21.6 feet and 20.9 feet, respectively. In intensity the storm was nearly as bad as the 1928 hurricane at Lake Okeechobee had been. The death toll was 51 people.

During October 9–16, 1947, a hurricane came across western Cuba into southwest Florida, then moving northeast into the Atlantic around Palm Beach. It was a Category 1 storm and was the first hurricane ever seeded.[1] It split in two in the Atlantic, and the worst part hit Savannah, Georgia.

There were two hurricanes in 1948. The first one ran from September 18 to 25 and was classified Category 3. The system started just west of Jamaica and moved west to northwest and then north over western Cuba into the Florida Straits. It struck Florida near Everglades City in the Ten Thousand Islands, moving northeast through Florida to emerge into the Atlantic near Jupiter. A tornado was reported in Homestead on September 21. Lowest barometric pressure was 28.44 inches, and top winds were 122 mph. The hurricane killed three people and caused $105 million in damage.

The second 1948 storm ran from October 3 to 5 and started just off the Nicaraguan and Honduran coast in the northwest Caribbean. This hurricane also moved across western Cuba into the Florida Straits and even crossed the September hurricane's path near the coordinates 24.0N and 82.0W. It passed through the Keys and extreme South Florida to cross Grand Bahama Island. At about 31°N latitude it made a gigantic loop in the middle of the Atlantic and finally became a nontropical cyclone. A tornado was reported in Fort Lauderdale on October 5. Lowest barometric pressure was 28.92 inches, and top winds were around 90 mph.

In August 1949 another major hurricane, taking a course similar to that of the Great Hurricane of September 1928, entered the coast near Palm Beach. It was the worst hurricane felt in the Lake Okeechobee area since 1928. Hurricane force winds were reported at St. Augustine, Cape Canaveral, and Melbourne, and winds of 120 mph or greater were felt from Stuart to Pompano. The highest recorded wind speed gust, 153 mph, was at Jupiter, only 2 mph less than the record set on September 27, 1947. The amount of damage in dollars, $45 million (equivalent to $270 million in 1990), was almost twice that of the 1928 hurricane. The storm was not classified as being among the Great Hurricanes in Florida's history, but it fell only slightly short of that category (U.S. Weather Bureau, August 1949). Tides were 24 feet and 23 feet at Belle Glade and Okeechobee, respectively.

By the time of the last two major hurricanes of the hectic decade 1941–50, storms were named using the World War II phonetic alphabet: Able, Baker, Charlie, Dog, Easy, etc.

Hurricane Easy, September 1950, Cedar Key

"Old residents say this was the worst hurricane in 70 years. . . . Half of the houses were severely damaged or destroyed. . . . The fishing fleet upon which the town depends for a livelihood, was completely destroyed by wind and waves. . . . The tide in Tampa Bay rose 6.5 feet, the highest since 1921" (U.S. Weather Bureau, 1950).

This hurricane looped twice on the west coast, had top winds of 125 mph, and showed barometric pressure of 28.30 inches. It brought 38.7 inches of rain to Yankeetown during September 5–6 and provoked residents of the area to unfounded accusations of seeding by the Weather Bureau.

Hurricane King, October 1950, Miami

The path of principal destruction was only 7–10 miles wide through the greater Miami area and northward to West Fort Lauderdale on October 17. It was at first reported that the damage was the result of a tornado or tornadoes, but careful inspection revealed no evidence of tornado action. This was simply a small, violent hurricane. Gusts were 150 mph at Miami and 138 mph at Fort Lauderdale. Barometric pressure fell to 28.20 inches, and tides were 19.3 feet at Clewiston. Three people died during this storm. The following eyewitness report on Hurricane King is by coauthor John M. Williams:

> This storm, Hurricane King, formed down in the northwest Caribbean not too far from Swan Island. It curved its way northward to clip the west tip of Jamaica. From there King traveled almost due north across Cuba to slam into Florida close to Miami and made passage through western Fort Lauderdale. I was home on leave from army duty on October 17, 1950, visiting my folks, who lived in Country Club Estates, which is now Plantation. This was my first hurricane on land. I had been in one on a ship at sea coming back from Occupation Duty in Europe. In the afternoon of the seventeenth, rain was coming intermittently in sheets and the wind was gusting pretty high. Then, as if nothing was going on, it would calm down and the sun would come out. We were from Iowa where when it looked stormy, you were going to get it! That, I found out, didn't mean anything down here in Florida. My mother had two cats, which were progressively getting noisy and mean. We found out later that they were affected by the barometric pressure drop as the storm approached. By the time the storm hit they were climbing the walls! The house was CBS block construction so we felt okay because shutters had been installed some years before. On the front porch were aluminum jalousies.

The main part of King hit us in the late evening and it was really something, to me at least! The street in front of the house was gravel back then and the winds picked the rock up and blasted the front of the house! The noise on those aluminum jalousies was so bad we couldn't hear each other talk. There was a lot of lightning in the storm and we could see out through the shutters. We thought newspapers were flying all over the place until we realized that what we were seeing were not newspapers but tiles off the roof.

We went outside during the eye and I found out what everybody had always said about the eye: we could see stars, the moon, and a few clouds, and we could feel a slight breeze. We detected a smell that some said was ozone. But ozone is odorless. Nevertheless we experienced the "hurricane eye smell."

The famous backside of the hurricane came right away, and we rode out the remainder of the storm like we did the first part. Now the wind came from the other direction and it loosened up everything.

After the passage of Hurricane King we took a long look at the damage. Out of six fruit trees, only one was still standing. About half of the roof tiles were lost and would need to be replaced. The aluminum jalousies were dented and stripped of all paint. Debris could be seen all over the place. As the area was wooded in that period of time, trees were down here and there. A big tree, about two feet in diameter, took down the power and telephone lines. I had returned to Fort Benning by the time power had been restored. We heard that a tornado was running around in the eye of King and wiped out a trailer park in the town of Dania, south of us. Some people were killed due to King.

The last 10 years (1951–60) of the 30-year segment from 1931 to 1960 were marked by a sharp reduction in major hurricane activity; it was during this period, in 1953, that the Weather Bureau began giving hurricanes female names.

In October 1951, Hurricane How, as a tropical storm, crossed mid-Florida. In 1952, a tropical storm crossed south Florida in February. This system started in the Caribbean Sea about the second of February, moving through the Yucatan Channel and then northeast into the Florida Keys, Florida Bay, and Florida's southwest coast. In no time it was out in the Atlantic becoming an extratropical storm, all in a matter of about two days. Even though the system was very fast moving, gusts of 68–84 mph were recorded in the Miami area.

In 1953, Tropical Storm Alice struck northwest Florida in June. In August an unnamed storm crossed South Florida. In September another unnamed storm crossed north Florida and Hurricane Florence hit northwest Florida. Tropical Storm Hazel crossed mid-Florida in October to finish out 1953. In 1956, Hurricane Flossy struck northwest Florida in September. Two tropical storms hit the same region in 1957, one unnamed and the other named Debbie.

The unnamed tropical storm of 1957 in the southwest Gulf of Mexico made landfall just east of Apalachicola on June 8. Suwannee and adjacent counties had 15 inches of rain in 48 hours. There was heavy crop damage, particularly to tobacco and watermelons, and 100–200 families had to evacuate near the city of Perry. There were at least nine tornadoes in northeast Florida on June 8 because of the northeast track of the storm.

A Gulf of Mexico storm from June 7 to 9, 1957, Debbie made landfall near Fort Walton Beach on June 8. Peak winds were 52 mph near Tampa and the low pressure reading was 29.68 inches in Pensacola. Wewahitchka recorded 11.26 inches of rain. There was flooding in St. Marks, but most of the rain was welcome because of the low levels of water in the lakes. In October 1959 two more tropical storms came ashore in Florida: Irene into northwest Florida and Judith crossing mid-Florida. Neither of these storms was of major consequence.

In 1960 Brenda crossed North Florida in September as barely a tropical storm, and Florence, also a weak storm, had crossed the south and central parts of the state a week earlier, but Hurricane Donna stole the show (fig. 4.A–C). Prior to Hurricane Andrew in 1992, Hurricane Donna ranked fifth among the most intense hurricanes to strike the United States during the twentieth century (Hebert et al., 1995). Except for the western Panhandle, where Flossy with a barometric pressure of 28.93 inches affected Pensacola in 1956 with gusts at 98 mph, Donna was the first major hurricane to have an effect on Florida since Hurricane King in 1950. It caused $300 million ($1.9 billion in 1990 dollars) in damages to the state and was one of the most destructive hurricanes to affect Florida in modern times (Dunn and Miller, 1964; Hebert et al.,

1995). In 1992 Hurricane Andrew replaced Donna as Florida's most damaging storm.

At Conch Key, pressure during Donna was 27.46 inches on September 10, 1960, and tides were 13 feet some 40 miles northeast and 20 miles southwest. Donna was at its peak here, moving at only 8 mph. The storm killed three people in the Keys. Top winds of 180–200 mph were recorded in the Keys, with gusts to 150 mph at Everglades City and Naples. (Recorded is "recorded by instrument.") Gusts are estimates and can be 20–40 percent higher than sustained winds. In central Florida, the pressure was 28.60 inches at Lakeland, 28.66 inches at Orlando, and 28.73 inches at Daytona. In Fort Myers the barometric pressure was 28.05 inches. Fifty people died when a U.S. airliner crashed off Dakar, Africa, at the beginning of the storm.

U.S. Weather Bureau records (September 1960) reflect the widespread damage:

> Storm damages range from very severe in the Middle Keys and the southwest coast from Everglades City to Punta Gorda, to relatively minor in northwest Florida and points north of the storm track. At Naples tides pushed inland to the center of the city damaging buildings and smashing docks all along the intrusion. Everglades City, a town that had been largely evacuated was also inundated by storm tides and about 50 percent of the buildings in that city were destroyed by tides and winds. Even well outside these areas, the wind toppled thousands of trees, demolished many weaker buildings, blew off or damaged roofs, and shattered many windows. Power and communication facilities fell throughout central and south Florida. Grapefruit losses were between 25 and 35 percent of the state's crop. Gusts of 99 mph recorded at the FAA tower in Daytona Beach marked Donna's exit from Florida, having retained hurricane status throughout its entire passage in Florida.

Donna inflicted major ecological damage. Dunn and Miller (1964) reported that 50 percent of one of the world's largest stands of mangrove trees was wiped out and that 35–40 percent of the white heron population was killed. In Everglades National Park, a monument on the road to Flamingo reminds visitors today about Hurricane Donna.

1961–1990

There were 25 storms during this 30-year segment. Comparing these figures with the 22 hurricanes and 29 tropical storms for the previous 30 years shows the overall reduction in both hurricanes and tropical storms (table 3). In the years from 1961 through 1992, six hurricanes in Category 3 or higher occurred—Betsy, Inez, Eloise, David, Elena, and Andrew—compared to 11 from 1931 to 1960. Hurricanes Inez and Kate did strike Florida but were Categories 1 and 2 storms at those stages; Inez and David were Category 4 storms in the Caribbean. Hurricanes Juan and Elena, in 1985, affected northwest Florida without a landfall.

During the first 10-year period, 1961–70, seven hurricanes—Cleo, Dora, Isbell, Betsy, Inez, Alma, and Gladys—hit Florida, a sharp increase over the previous 10 years, 1951–60. While there were no storms from 1961 to 1963, three hurricanes struck Florida in 1964 alone, making that year the costliest up to that date in Florida's history ($350 million and more, equivalent to $1.75 billion dollars in 1990).

In 1962 Alma passed Florida's east coast as a tropical depression on August 26. In 1965, a tropical storm crossed northwest Florida on June 15 from the Pacific.

Hurricanes Cleo and Isbell, 1964

In late August 1964, Hurricane Cleo was the first hurricane to strike the Miami area since Hurricane King in 1950. Cleo moved up the peninsula about 20 miles inland, paralleling the east coast. It produced 138 mph gusts at Bahia Mar Marina, Fort Lauderdale, and knee-deep water was observed in some locations. Due to its small size, Cleo soon weakened to below hurricane strength around the Fellsmere-Melbourne area, yet the total storm damage was estimated at $125 million ($600 million in 1990 dollars). Cleo sailed through Georgia, South Carolina, and North Carolina to break into the Atlantic in September. The storm regained hurricane status on the September 2 but died in the North Atlantic near Nova Scotia on September 5. According to the U.S. Weather Bureau report of August 1964, the main losses in Hurricane Cleo were from glass and water damage in the Miami Beach area and agricultural losses in the Indian River Lagoon citrus belt.

John Williams provided the following personal account of Cleo; its track in southeast Florida can be seen in semi-hourly records in figure 5.

Cleo was the worst in the southeast coastal area. Cleo was of Cape Verde vintage and traveled through the Atlantic and the Caribbean as a "textbook" storm. Between Jamaica and Haiti, however, she turned northward into the Guantanamo Naval Base in Cuba, causing considerable damage there and elsewhere in Cuba. Passing across Cuba brought the usual decrease in strength, but once into the Florida Straits she regained her hurricane status. My eyewitness report on the passage of Cleo is from the western Fort Lauderdale area.

There were winds and rain all day on August 26. Some gusts were in the 60 mph category. It seems that I had the only ladder in the neighborhood and since the people there knew I was in the weather business, a line of them formed as I was finishing the preparations on my house. I didn't see the ladder again until after the storm had passed, but I heard it got as far as two blocks away.

I knew the storm was going to hit this area after dark, so we decided to have supper and get all the other amenities out of the way. We put all the kids to bed early but that didn't last for long; after all, it was their first hurricane! It was lucky that we toweled up all the doors and had the shutters on the windows because at the height of the storm we had water coming in the front door and through some of the windows. We had glass jalousies throughout the house!

The storm peaked late in the evening just before the eye passage with gusts to 130 mph at my location, and there was considerable lightning, along with that tremendous roar. You could see almost like daylight through the shutters.

My children will never forget the "little leaf," obviously sheltered by the house, hopping across the yard, in the opposite direction from the wind. About ten minutes before the eye, a Florida room aluminum shutter, about 3 by 8 feet, ripped off the house next to mine. It slammed into the corner of my house and ricocheted out into my front yard. I had a small palm tree out there that was bending over from the winds, and the shutter managed to wedge itself between the bent tree and the ground.

The eye passage lasted one hour and twelve minutes at my location.

I opened the door at that time to a rush of water about 2 inches deep. While my wife mopped that up, I stepped off the porch into nearly knee-deep water and waded to the palm tree. As hard as I tried, I couldn't free the shutter from the tree.

I could see the stars in a beautiful sky about me and there was that unmistakable stillness and smell that only happens in the eye of a hurricane.

The guy across the street yelled over to me that he had lost all the glass jalousies from his Florida room and had to move inside the house. He had only taped his windows! I tugged again and again at the tree and big shutter but to no avail. I couldn't move it. I checked around the house and everything seemed all right or passable. But now it was time to get back inside the house because the backside of a hurricane comes on like gangbusters.

Since the wind comes from the opposite direction and right now, it is there before you know it! And it came. The palm tree straightened up and the big shutter came loose and was last seen, in lightning flashes, heading north, up over the house across the street. We never saw it again. The backside of the storm was drier than the front but not by much.

The house leaked (all houses leak in a storm like Cleo), and we had a lot of mopping to do. The pea-rock on the flat roof of the garage was all gone and there was a dent in the deck lid of our car parked in the carport; something was flying around loose. When the water subsided, it left a mass of debris all over the place, and power was off in some parts of town for five days. Our power came on again by late afternoon of August 27, one day after the storm passed by. There was widespread damage throughout the area but only an occasional catastrophic type.

In a few days, we had the place almost cleaned up; I had my ladder back and the kids still wanted to know what had happened to the little leaf. For a period after the storm when I mowed the lawn, the clippings were a combination of grass and pea-rock shrapnel.

In September 1964, just a few weeks after Hurricane Cleo, Hurricane Dora struck the Florida coast at St. Augustine from the east, at an angle near 90 degrees. It was the first hurricane to do so north of Stuart since the Great Hurricane of 1880. Winds of 125 mph at St. Augustine resulted in a 12-foot storm tide, which swept across Anastasia Island (St. Augustine) and also produced a 10-foot storm tide at Fernandina Beach and Jacksonville. These massive storm tides caused extensive beach erosion, inundated most beach communities, washed out beach roads, and swept buildings into the sea. There was also considerable flooding along the St. Johns River in Jacksonville. Total damage was estimated at $250 million dollars (more than $1 billion in 1990 dollars), according to the U.S. Weather Bureau (September 1964).

Hurricane Isbell, while not a strong hurricane, struck Florida in October 1964 and is described in an eyewitness account by John Williams:

This storm grew down south of the western tip of Cuba and proceeded northeast, across Cuba, the Florida Straits, and into the Ten Thousand Islands region of southwest Florida. From there, Isbell took a more northeast course across Florida. On the evening of October 14, the storm passed just northwest of Fort Lauderdale. Winds were 50 to 60 mph with a recorded gust of 120 mph. Many tornadoes spawned by Isbell caused as much damage as the hurricane did. Rains were extremely heavy in the early period of the storm but slacked off to nearly dry conditions at the end. Less than a block from where I lived, a tornado tore the whole Florida room, constructed of block, off a house. Isbell passed out to sea between the cities of Palm Beach and Vero Beach and dissipated in the Atlantic.

Hurricane Betsy, September 1965

The following year, in September 1965, Hurricane Betsy, a Category 3 storm, struck extreme southern Florida from the east. Wind gusts up to 60 mph were reported as far north as Melbourne. In south Florida, an observer at Grassy Key reported winds of 160 mph before the anemometer was blown away at 7:15 A.M. on September 8. Storm tides of 6 to 8 feet and wave action caused considerable flooding between greater Miami and the Palm Beaches (fig. 6.A); rising waters flooded extensive sections of Key Biscayne, covering virtually all of the island (U.S. Weather Bureau, September 1965).

Hurricane Betsy was unique. It formed far out in the Atlantic around August 27 and was obviously a Cape Verde–type hurricane. After moving west for a few days, it developed an erratic course starting around Puerto Rico (Sugg, 1966). The path was a zigzag, generally in a northwest direction to a point about 300 miles almost due east of Cape Kennedy, as the cape was known in those days. The storm became stationary there for nearly two days, then suddenly moved in a south-southwest direction, which took it right into the central Bahamas. Just east of Nassau, Betsy stalled again. For 20 hours, winds of 120 to 140 mph buffeted the area, causing death and destruction.

John Williams's eyewitness report is about the passage of Betsy in western Fort Lauderdale (see fig. 6.B for the barometric record):

During September 7 we were intermittently pelted with rain and strong wind gusts. Nassau is only about 150 nautical miles from Fort Lauderdale, and since Betsy was a large hurricane, we were getting all sorts of weather in the area.

During the early morning of the eighth, we were getting rain in sheets with several gusts in the 125 mph category. Sustained winds easily hung at around 65 mph. Even though we did not experience the eye, things would calm down to almost sunshine conditions but this would not last long.

There was a lot of flooding and house seepage but not as bad as during Cleo. Betsy's eye, which was huge and about 40 miles in diameter, was south of us and our pressure bottomed out at 29.12 inches.

This combination of pelting rain and heavy winds continued all day long, and even at suppertime it was still not advisable to venture outside. Our power was off for more than ten hours and the usual mass of debris was all over the place. There was a lot of orange and grapefruit damage as well as damage to other crops; again most of the pea-rock was blown off the garage roof.

Our place was wet for a long time and I recorded more than 8 inches of rain for the passage period. When there is no break in the continuity of a storm (the eye), you get the effects all the time: more rains, more winds, more everything.

Hurricane Inez, 1966

Inez was a Cape Verde–type hurricane with a classic track through the Caribbean, across Haiti and Cuba, and into the Florida Straits. From there the storm earned the nickname "the Crazy One" at the National Hurricane Center. It took an extremely erratic course, first north, then south, then east, and finally west, so that people on all sides were biting their fingernails.

Before the storm died in the mountains near Tampico, Mexico, Inez had killed more than 1,500 people. Top winds recorded reached 190 mph, and air reconnaissance flights noted barometric pressure of 27.38 inches. At the time, these characteristics qualified it as a Severe hurricane; today it would be considered a strong Category 4 hurricane. John Williams's eyewitness report is of the passage of the storm in western Fort Lauderdale.

> My wife and kids had gone to bed early that night and I told them that Inez was heading northeast. As erratic as it had been though, I was going to stay up and keep a check on it. I was off duty, so there was nothing else to do, and I was a storm hunter anyway. I was glued to the weather radio, TV, barometer, and the rest of the instruments at my station. But as enthusiastic as I was about the whole thing, I was guilty of dozing off two or three times.
>
> The winds were gusting at more than 40 mph and I had pulled down the shutters just in case.
>
> At 8:00 A.M. on October 3, the pressure at the house had been 29.65 inches, temperature was 78°F, dew point was 78°F, humidity was 100 percent, winds were north at 29 mph sustained, and it was overcast with rain. Inez was 93 miles east-northeast of Miami, moving north-northeast at 7 mph. We had it made. At 1100, the storm was 75 miles west-northwest of Nassau, moving north-northeast.
>
> At 1400, it was stationary about 85 miles west-northwest of Nassau.
>
> At 2300, Inez was drifting slowly south-southwest, pushing 25-foot seas, as reported by a Coast Guard cutter. The southeast Florida coast had gusts of more that 55 mph. Enthusiastic as I was about the whole thing, I dozed a couple of times, even though I knew the storm was now coming our way.

At 0345 on October 4, I awoke to shutters rattling and pelting rain. Winds were gusting more than 60 mph. Barometer was 29.59 inches, temperature was 75°F, dew point was 73°F, humidity was 91 percent, and it was overcast with thunder and lightning!

At 0700, Inez was 45 miles southeast of Miami with winds of at least 85 mph and moving west at 7 mph.

At 1100, the storm was moving west-southwest at 8 mph with gale force winds 175 miles to the north and 100 miles south. Here, we had hurricane gusts frequently and gales with heavy rains all day. U.S. Highway 1 in the Keys was underwater. The eye of the storm was 30 miles in diameter.

At 0200, my barometer was reading 29.67 inches and the wind was still gusting in excess of 45 mph.

By 1500 on October 5, Inez was stationary near Dry Tortugas with winds of 120 mph. From there, she finally continued west to Mexico.

We got a bit of minor damage on the house and there was a lot of trash to pick up around the yard. Everything was wet for a few days, but we considered ourselves lucky.

Until Hurricane Allison in 1995, Alma had the distinction of being the earliest storm to hit the United States during hurricane season. Alma struck northwest Florida on June 9, 1966, having started in the northwest Caribbean and tracked north across the western tip of Cuba on June 8. Landfall was about 20 miles east-northeast of Apalachicola. Winds of 76–100 mph were felt in the area. Pressure was 29.06 inches at Alligator Point. Tides of 4–10 feet hit the concave coastline in the area, and more than 6 inches of rain fell. Lowest pressure in the storm was 28.64 inches, and peak winds were 125 mph. Alma caused six deaths and $10 million in damages.

During October 18 and 19, 1968, Hurricane Gladys struck the west coast of Florida, arriving between Bayport and Crystal River about midnight on the eighteenth. Gladys formed in the western Caribbean near Swan Island and steadily moved on a northward track across western Cuba, over the Dry Tortugas, and over Florida's west coast.

Dry Tortugas and Plantation Key both reported winds near 90 mph. The storm's forward speed was about 15 mph. Tides along the west coast were 6.5 feet above normal, causing beach erosion and flooding, mostly between Clearwater and Bayport. Maximum gusts were over 100 mph and lowest pressure was 28.76 inches. Citrus was heavily damaged, and mobile home damage was extensive, as usual, as far inland as Ocala. Gladys broke out into the Atlantic near St. Augustine having killed three people in Florida and one person in Cuba. One more death was added in Nova Scotia, and the total damage was nearly $17 million in 1968.

On June 3, 1968, Abby was a Category 1 hurricane in the Gulf of Mexico heading for the Florida west coast. But on the morning of the fourth when it hit Punta Gorda, it was a tropical storm. During June 4 and 5 Abby headed east-northeast across Florida. Heavy rains brought relief from a drought; Titusville and Orlando recorded 10 inches of rain. Four tornadoes were reported near Pineda Bar and Haines City on the fourth. The system stalled along the beaches from Cape Kennedy to Jacksonville, producing winds of 66–77 mph. Peak wind was 90 mph recorded by air reconnaissance, and lowest pressure was 28.50 inches, also reported by aircraft.

Brenda was a depression in June passing through Florida. Dolly was a Category 1 hurricane in August in the Florida Straits but weakened to a depression as it dumped 2–4 inches of rain on southeast Florida and the Miami area.

The big storm in 1969 was, of course, Hurricane Camille, a Category 5 hurricane that ravished the upper Gulf Coast. Florida was lucky that year, suffering only from Tropical Storm Jenny. This was an early October storm making landfall near Naples on the second. Winds of 55 mph winds and pressure of 29.52 inches were good for up to 5 inches of rain over Florida. The slow-moving storm got to the Cape Kennedy area before moving back to the west and emerging into the Gulf on October 6.

In 1970 came another Alma (the name had been used in 1966 as well). Although only a depression through Florida, Alma nevertheless dumped more than 6 inches of rain on Fort Myers in 12 hours. Landfall was near Cedar Key on the May 25. Alma was only the third tropical storm in May in 100 years.

Becky arrived in July 1970. Landfall of this tropical storm was near Port St. Joe on July 22 with 63 mph winds and pressure of 29.62 inches. Nine inches of rain fell in the area, and a tornado destroyed three houses in Panacea, Florida. Tides in that area were 6 feet and damages $500,000. Greta was another 1970 storm, passing through the lower Keys on September 27 with 55 mph winds and pressure of 29.69 inches. Tavernier, to the northeast, recorded 55 mph winds. Rain was not unusually heavy.

Hurricanes Agnes, Eloise, and David, 1970s

The period from 1971 through 1980 had the lowest storm total of any decade the 130-year history considered—three hurricanes and one tropical storm. The three Florida hurricanes were Agnes, Eloise, and David.

Hurricane Agnes in 1972 was barely a Category 1 hurricane in Florida but resulted in major devastation in the middle, southern, and northeastern states and caused 122 deaths and $6 billion in damage (in 1990 dollars). It struck the Florida Panhandle and then merged with another system in mid–United States, triggering torrential rains and extreme flooding throughout the entire eastern seaboard. The threat of a hurricane usually diminishes rapidly as it moves inland and loses its oceanic heat source. Sometimes, however, a storm encounters an environment that supplies an auxiliary source of energy to maintain strength far inland. Such was the case with Agnes.

Agnes made landfall in the Florida Panhandle, near Apalachicola; Florida's losses were less than $10 million. But then it joined another system in the middle of the country and traveled nearly a thousand miles more, triggering torrential rains and extreme flooding throughout the entire eastern seaboard. It became one of the most destructive storms in U.S. history.

Hurricane Eloise in September 1975 was a Category 3 hurricane. Hurricane David in September 1979 had weakened from a Category 4 to a Category 2 hurricane when it struck Florida, but it still causesd over $400 million in damages.

Hurricane Eloise was a Category 3 hurricane. It made landfall about midway between Fort Walton Beach and Panama City and was the area's first direct hit by a major hurricane in the twentieth century. Measurements of high-water marks by the U.S. Army Corps of Engineers indicated hurricane tides of 12–16 feet above mean sea level. Eglin

Air Force Base, 20 miles west of the center, reported the highest sustained wind of 81 mph when the instrument failed; 14.9 inches of rain fell. However, maximum sustained winds were estimated at about 125 mph, with gusts to 156 mph. The lowest barometric pressure was 28.20 inches. The combined effects of winds and tides undermined or demolished numerous structures along the beach from Fort Walton Beach to Panama City. Damage was over $1 billion in 1990 dollars, and there were 21 deaths in the United States.

In August 1976, Tropical Storm Dottie formed in the Keys from a depression in the Gulf of Mexico. The system moved southeast, then east through the Keys on August 19, then north up the Florida southeast coast. Dottie came back out into the Atlantic later on the nineteenth near Palm Beach. Eight inches of rain and 3- to 5-foot tides were the result in the Miami area.

In 1979, the National Hurricane Center decided to integrate male and female names for the hurricanes in the Atlantic for the first time. Bob was the first Atlantic hurricane with a male name. David soon followed. Hurricane David in September 1979 had weakened from Category 4 to Category 2 when it struck Florida but nevertheless caused over $400 million in damage. It moved inland south of Melbourne on the east coast and then northward along the Indian River Lagoon to exit at New Smyrna Beach. This was the first hurricane to strike the Cape Canaveral area since the hurricane of 1926. Severe beach erosion from a storm tide of nearly 5 feet was reported in Brevard County and the southern portion of Volusia County. Some homes, businesses, and public buildings were severely damaged or destroyed; however, although damage was widespread, most was minor because the strongest winds were just offshore over the Atlantic Ocean.

Figure 7.A shows Hurricane David from the 22,000-mile-high Geosynchronous Operational Environmental Satellite (GOES) orbiting the earth. At this point on August 31, David was about to make landfall on Hispaniola, at about 6:00 P.M. EST. Winds were near 150 mph and the central pressure was 27.34 inches. Earlier, David had reached its peak when about 125 miles south of Puerto Rico, with sustained winds of 150 mph and central pressure of 27.29; at that time it rated as a Category 4 hurricane.

On September 1 at 6:00 A.M., David broke into the sea north of Hispaniola and Haiti. Winds were down to about 75 mph after crossing a 10,000-foot mountain in the Dominican Republic. Later that day, a hurricane watch was posted for South Florida, with the weakened storm some 350 miles southeast of Miami. Late that evening hurricane warnings went out as the now strengthened hurricane, with 90 mph winds, was 300 miles from Miami.

At 7:00 A.M. on September 3 David was 35 miles east of Fort Lauderdale, with 85 mph winds and pressure of 28.85 inches. Fort Lauderdale experienced torrential rain in squalls with gusts of over 75 mph. Since the eye and strong side of the storm were over the ocean, this condition persisted for most of the day.

Figure 7.B shows David at about 6:00 that evening. The storm made landfall about 20 miles south of Melbourne with 90 mph winds and central pressure of 28.75 inches, a Category 2 hurricane. From there it reached Savannah, Georgia, before downgrading to a tropical storm on September 4. By the seventh David was no longer a threat, and it died near Newfoundland (see fig. 7.C). Fatalities were five in the United States, seven in Puerto Rico, 56 in Dominica, and 1,200 in the Dominican Republic. The damage was $5 million (1990 dollars) in the United States, including Florida.

While Hurricane Frederic in August–September 1979 did not strike Florida directly, hurricane warnings extended over to Panama City on September 11, and gale warnings were displayed south to Cedar Key. Frederic had a development that was similar to David's, causing much apprehension because people were not ready for another storm so soon, just one week after David.

The final decade under review in this chapter marked an upswing in overall storm activity (table 3). Some of the storms became hurricanes after they passed Florida and are mentioned briefly here.

On August 17–18, 1981, Tropical Storm Dennis struck Florida. Dennis started as a tropical storm southwest of the Cape Verde Islands on August 6; it continued at this level near Barbados but became a tropical depression south of Puerto Rico and then turned into a mere disturbance. Just west of Jamaica, Dennis regained tropical storm status, turned north, and slammed into the southwest Florida coast. It tracked up through central Florida to become stationary between Fort Myers and southwest Lake Okeechobee. Southeast Florida had 10 inches of rain and Homestead 20 inches. Winds were more than 55 mph. Finally, Dennis moved across the lake and out to sea near Melbourne and Cape Canaveral. On August 20, east of Cape Hatteras, Dennis became a hurricane.

On August 25, 1983, Tropical Storm Barry struck Florida, crossing the state on a track from Melbourne to Tampa, first as a tropical storm and then as a tropical depression. After crossing the Gulf, Barry became a hurricane southeast of Brownsville, Texas, on August 28.

Hurricane Diana, which gained hurricane status on September 10, 1984, scraped the Florida coast between Daytona and Jacksonville on September 9–10 as a tropical storm; winds were in excess of 70 mph.

Tropical Storm Isidore occurred during the period between September 25 and October 1, 1984. On the twenty-seventh, it had winds of 50 mph. Landfall occurred between Vero Beach and Melbourne that evening. From there the storm went to Orlando at about midnight, then traveled west to about 75 miles north of Tampa. On the twenty-eighth it made another turn and headed northeast, crossing over to Jacksonville and then out to sea; the storm was accompanied by heavy rains.

Hurricane Bob, relatively short lived, struck the southwest Florida coast near Fort Myers on July 21–25, 1985, as a tropical storm. Winds were 50–70 mph. It crossed Lake Okeechobee and went out to sea near Vero Beach on July 23, whereupon it took a sharp turn to the north, skirting Daytona on July 24. Bob became a hurricane at sea that day, east of Georgia.

On October 9–13, 1987, Hurricane Floyd appeared. It moved across the western tip of Cuba on October 11 on a northeast track. It made a more easterly turn across the Dry Tortugas and into the Keys on October 12, becoming a hurricane near Key West with winds of 80 mph. The eye crossed over Key West at about noon. Warnings were given all across South Florida; some tornadoes occurred on the southwest coast.

The eye of the storm appeared over Marathon later and over Key Largo at about 6:00 P.M. Floyd's winds were 75 mph and the barometric pressure was 29.32 inches. About 30 miles south of Miami, Floyd broke out into the Atlantic near midnight on October 12. Winds and rain attributed to Floyd were felt as far as Palm Beach.

Hurricanes Elena, Juan, and Kate all occurred in 1985. Elena, a Category 3 hurricane in August–September, deserves discussion although it never actually made landfall in Florida (fig. 8). Its center passed within 40 miles of the west coast, where it stalled for about 24 hours offshore from Cedar Key, then moved west-northwest, passing within 30 miles of Cape San Blas. The storm tide created during this hurricane's passage caused heavy waterfront damage in the City of Cedar Key and the disappearance of 1,500 feet of the exposed south tip of Cape San Blas. Because of the offshore location of Elena's peak winds, most of the damage to the coast was due to the storm tide (7–9 feet) and wave activity causing destruction, which stretched from Venice to Pensacola. Nearly a million people were evacuated from low-lying coastal sections in the warning areas posted for Hurricane Elena.

While also not striking the Florida coastline directly, Juan in October–November 1985 nevertheless impacted the extreme northwest Florida Panhandle (fig. 9.A–C). Pinellas, Manatee, Sarasota, and Lee counties were continuously pounded by the storm's spiral bands through the evening of Halloween.

On November 21, 1985, Hurricane Kate, a Category 2 storm, struck the coast near Port St. Joe in the Florida Panhandle (fig. 10.A–B). It was the only hurricane to strike Florida so late in the season this far north. Just prior to making landfall near Mexico Beach, about halfway between Panama City and Port St. Joe, Kate slowed in forward speed and weakened in the early morning because of cooler sea surface temperatures in the northern Gulf of Mexico. The total damage was mainly due to the storm tide and wave activity. Some $300 million in damage (1990 dollars) resulted, yet it caused only about one-fourth of the damage inflicted by Hurricane Elena (table 4).

Tropical storm Isabel scraped extreme northeast Florida near Fernandina Beach and the Florida-Georgia border on October 10, 1985, with minimal damage. Hurricane Chris was a tropical storm when it visited Florida during August 1988. It skirted the east coast from Miami to Jacksonville, first as a tropical depression, then as a tropical storm on August 27 and 28, bringing heavy rains. Hurricane Keith was a tropical storm during November 17–24, 1988. It moved over Florida's west coast between Fort Myers and Tampa on November 22 as a tropical storm with 65 mph winds. The storm crossed the state intact and came out into the Atlantic near Melbourne and Cape Canaveral on November 23. Heavy rains fell and some tornadoes were sighted.

While 1990 produced 14 named storms—the most since naming began in 1953—only Marco, a tropical storm, affected the northwest portion of Florida slightly, and Klaus, as a final disturbance, got into the central and north-central part of Florida.

Note

1. Seeding is the introduction of dry ice or silver iodide into a storm for the purpose of reducing its strength by cooling. It was not successful and is not done any more. The seeding may or may not have been the cause of the split.

3

Four Years and Billions of Dollars Later,
1991–1994

The even-numbered years of this four-year period provided the most activity in Florida. Hurricane Andrew in 1992 dominated the period with more than $30 billion in damages. In 1994, Alberto, Beryl, and Gordon chalked up more than $1 billion in damages as tropical storms. Although the population and building densities involved for these storms were lower than during Hurricane Andrew and the dollar value of damage was commensurately lower, the three certainly underscored that one should not underestimate "mere" tropical storms.

The 1991 Season

The hurricane season of 1991 produced no more than a brush with Tropical Storm Fabian on the extreme southeast tip of Florida. Hurricane Bob, the most potent of the 1991 season, initially headed toward the Miami–Palm Beach area but executed a turn of almost 90 degrees when 200 to 300 miles off the coast and missed all of Florida. The Sunshine State escaped once again.

The 1992 Season

Hurricane Andrew

Except for several tropical depressions, June, July, and half of August in the 1992 hurricane season were quiet. The last season with a late start had been 1977, with Anita on August 28, in the Gulf of Mexico.

But on August 14, 1992, satellite photos indicated a strong tropical wave off the African coast in the area of the Cape Verde Islands. This system moved west for two days and developed into a tropical depression near 11.6N and 40.4W early on August 17. By noon that day the winds had reached 40 mph and Tropical Storm Andrew was named. Its position was about 1,175 miles east of the Lesser Antilles.

By August 20, Andrew was in trouble. The winds were less than 45 mph and the barometric pressure was that of normal sea level, leaving the whole system shaky. At this point San Juan, Puerto Rico, was only 350 miles southwest of the storm, but Andrew had slowed down.

The next morning, however, winds were up to 60 mph and pressure had dropped to 29.71 inches. By 11:00 that night, Andrew was 610 miles east of Nassau in the Bahamas, with 65 mph winds. On the morning of August 22, air reconnaissance confirmed that "Andrew is now a hurricane." Winds were 76 mph, pressure was 29.35 inches, and the storm was 800 miles east of Miami. At 11:00 that night Andrew was moving dead west at 15 mph with 110 mph winds and a pressure of 28.32 inches—a Category 2 hurricane.

By noon of August 23 Andrew had intensified to become a Category 4 hurricane. Winds were 135 mph, pressure had dropped to 27.46 inches, and the storm was 330 miles east of Miami, still moving west at 16 mph. At 2:25 that afternoon, Andrew was at its peak with 150 mph winds and pressure of 27.23 inches (Andrew came close to being a Category 5 storm). At this point a hurricane watch was posted from Titusville south to Vero Beach, and hurricane warnings covered the area from Vero Beach south through the Keys and up the west coast to Fort Myers.

By 9:00 in the evening on August 23, Andrew was in the Bahamas, 180 miles east of Miami. Landfall near Miami was predicted for the early morning of August 24. Indeed, between 4:00 and 5:00 A.M. that morning Andrew struck the Florida coastline just south of Miami with sustained winds of 145 mph and recorded gusts of 164 mph, as reported by the National Hurricane Center in Coral Gables before the main radar at the center was destroyed (color plate 1). Gusts to 175 mph were later confirmed.

Andrew crossed the state with 125 mph winds and a forward speed of 18 mph, still moving dead west and by now a Category 3 storm (fig. 11.A). Pressure was 27.91 inches. According to the U.S. Army Corps of

Engineers (1993), some recorded gusts in mph were Fowey Rocks (Biscayne Bay), 169; National Hurricane Center, 164; Turkey Point Power Plant, 163; Turkey Point Nuclear Power Plant, 160; Miami International Airport, 115; Goodyear Blimp Base at Pompano, 100; Palm Beach International Airport, 54. Once over the warm waters of the Gulf of Mexico, winds returned to 140 mph, back to Category 4.

By 6:00 A.M. on August 25, Andrew was 270 miles southeast of New Orleans, now moving west-northwest at 17 mph. Winds were 140 mph. At 1:00 P.M. that day the storm was 150 miles south of New Orleans, moving west-northwest at 16 mph. Winds were still 140 mph and barometric pressure 27.85 inches.

The storm slowed down to almost stationary 30 miles southeast of Lafayette, Louisiana. Early on the twenty-sixth, winds near New Iberia, Louisiana, were reported to be 115 mph with gusts to 160 mph. Landfall occurred between New Iberia and Lafayette, as a Category 3 hurricane. By noon on August 26 Andrew was downgraded to tropical storm status for the first time since August 22. Near Baton Rouge, Louisiana, up to 10 inches of rain fell and there were 65 mph winds, with tornadoes. The system was in eastern Tennessee by the morning of August 28, trying to merge with a cold front, the remains of the Pacific hurricane Lester. Andrew finally died out in Pennsylvania on August 29, 1992.

On Sabbatical with Hurricane Andrew

After anchoring their 40-foot sailboat named *Sabbatical* in Manatee Bay in the upper Keys, Dr. Thomas Stephens, dean of the School of Aeronautics at the Florida Institute of Technology in Melbourne, and his wife, Lois, took refuge in a friend's home in southwest Miami. The following eyewitness account is by Lois Stephens.

> Sleep was difficult, but I think we all managed to sleep some. About 2:00 A.M. it started. The wind was howling and shutters were banging. The five of us all crowded into the hallway, just like the usual pre-hurricane instructions stated. Fortunately, Karen had put out candles for us. So far, so good.
>
> The lights went out; the rain started. The wind got many times stronger and the house almost shivered. The force became so great we ran almost panicky into the bathrooms. There were two, both

without windows. Ron and Karen headed for one, Lee, Tom and I the other. We sat on lawn chairs, nestled close together, in the dark with our eyes closed. We opened the door only long enough to get a small votive candle, but the force became too great to open it. The wind grew more ferocious. Suddenly, the windows began to blow out, one at a time, fiercely smashing against the tiled floors. One huge crash I assumed to be the TV, but it was the newly purchased computer. Glass kept smashing. I had been aware for some time of my two root canals. It was strange, but the teeth had piercing pain. I remembered once before being in an airplane with inadequate pressure regulation and experiencing the same pain. Then it hit.

The drop in pressure in the house was so intense it caused pain in your ears and you had to keep swallowing, something like when a plane takes off, but much, much worse. We tried to open the bathroom door, but the force was too great. So three and two of us sat in silence, eyes closed, waiting for the horror to end. The small door to the "attic" storage space blew in and the rain followed. Water crept in around our feet, and I had a dread of it rising. But it did not. Sometime after 6:00, I think, the wind subsided substantially, and we had nerve enough to leave our sanctuary.

The house was all but demolished. The bed where Tom and I had slept a few hours before was full of glass and wet soggy debris. (My emergency bag of clothing, etc., was waterproof, but I had left it unzipped so it was likewise wet and full of junk.) The newly tiled (and in three rooms, newly carpeted) floors were covered with roof shingles, nails, much glass of all sizes, furniture, books, and of course, with a couple of inches of water. Ceiling fans still clung to their mountings, but under each, the light globes were full of dirty water. Water oozed from holes in the walls where Karen's newly framed tropical paintings had been hung (she is an artist). Paint was stripped from the walls. The carport (a sturdy "permanent" one) and door overhang were gone. The new roof was without shingles, and had gaping holes. A look outside showed that all trees and fences were down.

It was, of course, light now, so being cautious but ignoring some of the warnings we had heard, we walked around the neighborhood. It was sickening, horrifying. Not one house had escaped major damage. Trees, even the largest, were sprawled over houses, cars, and streets. Some cars had only broken windows and dents (as did our friend's), and some were blown about and overturned. One had burned from a fallen power line. Not just the power lines were down, but heavy-duty power poles were also broken. Except for no smoke or fires at this point, it must have been what a "bombed out" area looks like in wartime.

Miraculously, quick checks with neighbors found no one injured. Since roads in every direction were impassable, any hope of getting back to what might or might not be left of our boat were given up for the present.

[Later] Highways were somewhat clear by this time, except for some questionable power lines. Trees and large downed poles lined the way. What was most amazing, though, was that literally thousands of cars had found their way to the same area where we were. Traffic was next to impossible, lights and signs inoperative, and cars in extremely questionable condition. We'll never know the number of traffic accidents that day alone.

We passed the hotel, the Holiday Inn, where we had tried so desperately to get a room. It was standing, but barely, with all windows, balconies, etc., blown away. We passed houses with walls only and houses without any walls. Devastation went on for miles. We passed lines of hundreds of people waiting for water. Huge trucks had apparently been placed there at some point to distribute bottled water. One truck had blown uselessly on its side.

Eventually we got to our boat—it was not where we had left it, of course, but it looked good and was tightly nestled back in a grove of mangroves, aground. Miraculously, even the little Zodiac dinghy was still tied to it, snuggled alongside like a loyal puppy nestled against its master. A window was out, glass was everywhere, and branches were entwined in some lines. A stanchion (Tom says) was out and leaves and red mud covered one side of the boat. It was beautiful—we were ecstatic. The carpet was wet—the galley was soaked and covered with glass, but everything else was as we left it.

That night, Tom and I were alone in the middle of Manatee Bay, the most beautiful anchorage of our entire sailing experience.

The sky was clear and bursting with stars with no electric lights to distract from their beauty. There were no airplanes, distant cars, trains, or any noises. The most amazing phenomenon was taking place in the water around us. We had seen luminous fish on occasion, but we saw intensely brilliant green fish swimming around the boat. We dropped a line in the water and swirled it around and it left a trail of light behind it, somewhat like a comet. If we splashed the water, we splashed thousands of tiny lights. (All of this, of course, sent us later to our reference books to see what we had discovered.) We were so fortunate, so thankful, and we sipped our champagne.

[The next day] We were stopped by the Miami Police in a huge inflatable boat and advised we were on the Coast Guard "list" (missing persons and boats) and to call home."

Andrew Epilogue

The death toll in Hurricane Andrew was 24, far less than has occurred in past hurricanes of comparable strength. Massive evacuations ordered in Florida and Louisiana account for the low death rate.

Hurricane Andrew was the most destructive natural disaster in U.S. history (fig. 11.B–I). Damage estimates outstripped $30 billion, most of the property losses being in southern Dade and Monroe counties, from Kendall southward to Key Largo; for the Bahamas the damage was estimated at $250 million and for Louisiana more than $1 billion. In Dade County 90 percent of all homes had major roof damage (U.S. Army Corps of Engineers, 1993), and 117,000 homes were destroyed or had major damage.

According to the U.S. Army Corps of Engineers, who worked cooperatively with other agencies to determine environmental impacts, 12.7 million cubic yards of debris resulting from Andrew were hauled away; there were 39 approved debris-burning sites. Florida's agricultural industry loss alone came to $1.04 billion. There was also moderate impact damage to the offshore reef areas down to a depth of 75 feet (U.S. Army Corps of Engineers, 1993).

Damage to the Turkey Point nuclear power plant belonging to Florida Power and Light Company was $100 million (U.S. Army Corps of Engineers, 1993). As to moored recreational vessels within Biscayne

Bay, a total of 918 hurricane-damaged vessels were found; "roughly . . . one-third of the damaged vessels were completely or partially submerged, damaged but floating, and damaged aground" (Antonini et al., 1993). The site of the greatest devastation was in the area of Dinner Key Marina near Coral Gables in Miami.

The recovery process is still under way, but it should be emphasized that the results of tremendous structural damage by Andrew's winds could become cumulative in the future.

Andrew was a compact system with maximum winds occurring in a radius of only about 12 miles. A larger system or one with a landfall a few miles farther north would have been even more catastrophic, affecting the more heavily populated areas of Greater Miami, Miami Beach, and Fort Lauderdale. New Orleans could also have fared much worse than it did.

As noted in chapter 2, Hurricane Andrew chalked up some weather records. The 16.9-foot storm tide in Biscayne Bay was a record maximum for southeast Florida. Louisiana had 7-foot storm tides. In the twentieth century, only Hurricane Camille in 1969 and the Great Labor Day Hurricane of 1935 in the Florida Keys had lower barometric pressures at landfall. Barometric pressure associated with Andrew bottomed out at 27.23 inches.

Andrew broke wind speed records. A maximum 10-second flight-level wind speed of 170 knots, or 196 mph, was reported by the reconnaissance aircraft in the vicinity of northern Eleuthera Island in the Bahamas on August 23. The storm surge there was 23 feet.

Andrew will not be the last hurricane to cause such massive devastation and havoc. A similar storm could appear next year, or ten years from now; there is no way to know when. However, the bitter lessons learned in Hurricane Andrew should provide us with ample experience to survive the next big one.

The 1993 Season

No hurricanes or tropical storms struck or seriously affected Florida in 1993. The most powerful storm of the season was Hurricane Emily, from August 22 to September 6. A Category 3 hurricane with top winds of 120 mph and low pressure of 28.38 inches, it came directly at Florida until August 28, at which time it turned to the northwest. Because Andrew in 1992 was still fresh in memory, Emily gave everyone on the coast from Miami to Jacksonville a first-class scare, but this storm never got to within 800 miles of the Florida coast at any stage. Emily scraped the Cape Hatteras area with minimal damage, then turned east again to die out some 480 miles south-southeast of Cape Race, Newfoundland.

The 1994 Season

Alberto, June 27–July 4

The 1994 Florida hurricane season started with a disturbance in the Bahamas near 23N and 78W on June 27. This system moved west through the Florida Straits, across Cuba, and into the Yucatan Channel. On June 29, it turned north and became a tropical depression (see tracking plate 13 and fig. 12.A for detailed track.) On July 1 winds were 40 mph, pressure was 29.74 inches, and Alberto was named when it was 425 miles southeast of the mouth of the Mississippi River. The next day, winds were up to 60 mph, pressure had fallen to 29.47 inches, and Alberto was 150 miles south of Pensacola. A slight turn to the north-northeast on July 3 steered it to a Florida landfall near Destin at about noon. Winds at landfall were 65 mph with peak gusts as high as 86 mph. The barometric pressure bottomed out at 29.32 inches. Maximum tides were more than 5 feet, and 5–10 inches of rain fell in the area.

Alberto, now a tropical depression, moved slowly to near Atlanta, where it became stationary for almost two days. A slow move to the south and southwest brought the system into southwest Georgia and north Florida. Heavy flooding in Georgia, Alabama, and Florida resulted in 13 counties being declared disaster areas in Florida alone. All rivers in northwest Florida and southern Georgia were over their banks. The Apalachicola, Chipola, Withlacoochee, Ochlockonee, and Flint rivers were all over flood stage (fig. 12.B–C). Up to 27.61 inches of rain fell in southern Georgia and extreme north Florida. Two thousand people were evacuated from the areas affected, and as many as 18,500 were without electricity for more than two days. Some 300,000 chickens and 125 steers and hogs as well as 50 percent of the peanut, cotton, soybean, and corn crops were destroyed. In Apalachicola Bay, 90 percent of the oyster beds were destroyed. There were 31 deaths, and damage was over $500 million. By July 6 Alberto was gone, leaving a saturated Florida Panhandle, Georgia, and Alabama. It was evidence that tropical storms can cause more damage than some hurricanes.

Beryl, August 13–17

The second tropical cyclone of the 1994 hurricane season also made Florida a target. A disturbance off the state's west coast near Sarasota was found moving northwest on August 13. Beryl was named as a tropical storm just off Cape San Blas (tracking plate 13, fig. 13). On August 15, the storm carried 58 mph winds and pressure of 29.71 inches while pushing 3–5 foot surges along the Panhandle coastline. Although the main track appeared to be northeast, the center oscillated first west and then east, finally making landfall near Panama City. Winds of 60 mph were felt at Shell Point, at Turkey Point, and at the state capitol at Tallahassee. Lowest pressure measured was 29.50 inches at landfall. Tallahassee, still soaked from Alberto, received 9 inches of rain, and Apalachicola got 10.69 inches. There was heavy flooding in Apalachicola and Cedar Key, and several dozen tornadoes were sighted in Florida, Georgia, the Carolinas, and Virginia. Twenty thousand people lost power for several days. The oyster beds in Apalachicola Bay were again hit hard and had to be closed due to contamination. By 6:00 A.M. on August 16, the system was 80 miles southwest of Albany, Georgia, moving northeast at 6 mph. It still packed 64 mph winds and pressure of 29.56 inches. By 6:00 that evening, Beryl was a depression in north-central Georgia, moving north-northeast at 15 mph and dissipating rapidly. Beryl caused no deaths but chalked up $73 million worth of damage. The Panhandle, still only half dried out after Alberto, had to start all over again.

In the meantime, the Atlantic was fairly busy with Hurricane Chris and Tropical Storms Debby and Ernesto, largely deep-Atlantic storms. September was hurricane-free for the first time since 1968. There was a suspicious area of low pressure in the mid-Gulf on the September 30, but nothing developed. Early November produced Hurricane Florence, a Category 2 storm in the Atlantic and the strongest of the season; based on the experience of the past, it was expected to be the last for the year.

Gordon, November 8–21

But on November 8, just off the Nicaraguan coast, Tropical Depression 12 formed and moved slowly north. On November 10, when the storm was about 50 miles off the Nicaraguan-Honduran coast, it became the seventh named storm of the 1994 season—Gordon (tracking plate 13, color plate 2, and fig. 14.A). The northerly track continued until November 12, when the system turned east. It stayed on this track south of Cuba until the thirteenth. Just south of the Guantanamo Naval Base, Tropical Storm Gordon turned north and passed over eastern Cuba into the Bahamas. On the November 14 it was moving west through the Florida Straits. Guantanamo recorded a peak gust to 120 mph (probably from one of the numerous thunderstorms).

On November 15 air reconnaissance reported the center to be near the north Cuban coast, while radar showed a new center forming about 25 miles east-southeast of Key West. Gordon was moving west at 6 mph with winds of more than 50 mph and pressure at 29.50 inches. Later that same day, Gordon turned north, putting the center about 110 miles south of Sarasota. A more northeasterly turn on the sixteenth put the landfall near Fort Myers about noon. During that day, the system, still a tropical storm, crossed Florida with sustained winds around 45 mph and heavy rains (fig. 14.B). It emerged into the Atlantic south of Melbourne around midnight.

Flooding from the heavy rains resulted in heavy crop damage. The entire potato crop in Dade County was submerged. Virginia Key recorded a sustained wind of 53 mph, and a peak gust of 83 mph was noted in another part of Dade County. From 6 to 9 inches of rain fell in most of Florida, with more than 16 inches in Broward County. Six tornadoes were confirmed in the state during the passage. One just south of Melbourne at Barefoot Bay killed one person and injured 40 more; seven people drowned along the southeast coast.

In Volusia County, 1,236 buildings were damaged and heavy flood damage was evident, mostly to roads and sewers. Power and telephone lines and signs were also heavily damaged. Some 425,000 customers were without power in Dade and Broward counties. A 506-foot-long freighter was beached off Fort Lauderdale, and 37 people were rescued from sinking boats. Gordon continued northeast into the Atlantic and became a hurricane about noon on November 17, some 325 miles south of Cape Hatteras, North Carolina. Highest winds were 85 mph with the pressure lowest at 28.94 inches (fig. 14C).

But this erratic storm was not finished. A counterclockwise loop brought Gordon back toward Florida, and on November 20, around midnight, the system was making landfall just north of Cape Canaveral as a depression, still with winds of 25–30 mph and heavy rains. Dissipation took place as the system moved through Florida and Georgia. The total damage was more than $400 million, and Gordon killed 1,145 people, most in Haiti.

On December 21, a low-pressure area formed near 24N and 86W in the Gulf of Mexico and moved east-northeast. This system crossed South Florida the same day and entered the Atlantic Ocean as a tropical system on the twenty-second. Fowey Rocks, Miami, and Lake Worth automated stations recorded 51 mph sustained winds at 6:00 P.M. on December 21, and Florida got 7 inches of rain during the passage. The storm was not named.

That brought to an end the 1994 hurricane season. There had been seven storms altogether—three hurricanes and four tropical storms. The season was unusual in view of the suppressed activity during the height of the season (August–October), and not since 1980 had there been two November hurricanes. No major hurricanes (Categories 3–5 on the Saffir/Simpson scale) occurred either, although the average is 2.1 storms of Categories 3–5 per season.

4

Allison to Roxanne, 1995

The 1995 hurricane season was not a record one, but it was a close second to the 1933 season, which had 21 storms. There were 19 named storms in 1995 (the average is nine), 11 of which became hurricanes (the average is six). All but two of the 19 storms in 1995 grew from tropical waves originating off the West African coast. The season cost the areas affected more than $9 billion in damage, and an estimated 128 lives were lost in the Atlantic Basin.

Of the 11 hurricanes, Felix, Luis, and Opal were Category 4 storms; Marilyn and Roxanne were Category 3; and there were two Category 2 and four Category 1 storms. Erin and Opal struck the Florida coast as hurricanes, and Allison and Jerry were tropical storms at Florida landfall. Florida had not been hit with four tropical storms in a single season since 1953, and the overall season has not been so busy since 1969.

Between them, Hurricane Erin and Tropical Storm Jerry inundated east-central Florida with more than 30 inches of rain. Opal went into the record books as the second most expensive storm in the state (Andrew holds that record). It caused major erosion along 57 miles of Panhandle beaches, where the costs of repair were estimated over $100 million. This exceeds erosion damage done by Andrew, Eloise, and other major storms in Florida. The Opal storm surge was estimated to be 12 to 15 feet in some areas, and beach dunes as high as 21 feet were flattened.

Allison, June 3–6

A disturbance was noted in the northwest Caribbean on the first of June. By the third, this system was a tropical depression 160 miles south of the western tip of Cuba, moving north-northwest at 10 mph. At 11:00 A.M. the storm was named Allison (fig. 15.A, tracking plate 13), the first named storm of the 1995 season. Winds were 40–45 mph, pressure was 29.59 inches, and the storm was moving north-northwest at 14 mph, heading for Cozumel and Yucatan in Mexico.

At 2:00 P.M., however, Allison was 70 miles east-southeast of Cancun on a northerly track at 15 mph. Early on June 4, the storm had cleared the Yucatan Channel, winds were up to 60 mph, and pressure had fallen to 29.41 inches. By noon Allison was a hurricane, 300 miles south of Apalachicola and moving north at 16 mph. This was the storm's peak, with 75 mph winds and pressure of 29.15 inches.

At 6:00 A.M. on June 5, Allison was 40 miles southwest of Apalachicola pushing high tides, spawning tornadoes, and dropping over 5 inches of rain. Landfall was near St. George Island, Florida, as a minimal hurricane or strong tropical storm. The system was large at this point, and actual landfall was between St. George Island and St. Marks (color plate 3). Heavy rains throughout the area caused flooding, and gusts up to 54 mph were felt as far north as North Carolina's Outer Banks. The remnants ended up in Massachusetts. Allison caused one death and $1.7 million in damage (fig. 15.B). It was the earliest storm to strike the Florida Panhandle in the twentieth century.

Tropical Storms Barry, Chantal, and Dean in July remained in the Atlantic and Gulf of Mexico and did not affect Florida.

Erin, July 31–August 6

Erin formed from Tropical Depression 5 in the southeast Bahamas (fig. 16.A, tracking plate 13). The system had been tracked from east of the Leeward Islands. The storm moved west-northwest at 10 mph and was about 340 miles east-southeast of Miami when it became Hurricane Erin, with winds of 75 mph and pressure of 29.21 inches.

At 6:00 A.M. on August 1, hurricane warnings were issued along Florida's southeast and central coast. By 1:00 in the morning on August

2, Erin was making landfall north of Vero Beach between Sebastian and Palm Bay, similar to Hurricane David's landfall in 1979. At that time pressure was 29.09 inches, and winds of more than 85 mph were occurring (color plate 4, fig. 16.B–C). John Williams describes the eye passing over his house in Palm Bay:

> The eye passage started at 0245, at which time the barometric pressure bottomed out at 29.00 inches [fig. 16.C]. Before that, it was the usual squally, hard rain–light rain routine of an approaching storm.
>
> Winds gusted to more than 65 mph at times and I watched sustained winds over 50 mph for as long as 20 minutes at a time. All this from the north. I was worried about my garage door (two-car garage), as this can be the weakest part of one's house—but I had parked my pickup truck close to and across the door. It shook and rattled but held up OK. During the eye, the sky was relatively clear with occasional light breezes. Once for about five minutes, nothing stirred!
>
> At 0330, the winds picked up rapidly from about 110 degrees and now there were several severe thunderstorms added to the other activities.
>
> My peak gust of 75 mph from 140 degrees came at 0404 and the worst part of the storm was definitely the back side. I measured more than 8.3 inches of rain during the passage, and more than 10 inches fell before the system was out of here.
>
> There was minimal damage, lots of debris; the power sputtered several times but never went off and I finally lost cable TV about 0530 after recording the whole storm. By 0700 Erin was dumping heavy rain on Disney World and still doing it locally. I had no flooding problems, but a few blocks away there were major flood problems plus the power was off there.

Iver Duedall, living in Melbourne Village a few miles north of Palm Bay, was in a position to give an eyewitness account of Erin's devastation:

> My wife, Mary, and I went to bed early on the evening of the August 1. We were awakened at about midnight by the sounds of thunder and lightning and strong gusts of wind hitting the palms

and pines. With outside floodlights on, we experienced our very first Florida hurricane inside the comfort of our house; the power went out at about 4:00 A.M., so we finished out the storm by candlelight.

The severity of the storm seemed to lessen by around 0430. The eye of the storm passed south of us, near John Williams's house in Palm Bay, so we really never experienced the "before and after the eye of a hurricane." Oh well, next time. When it came light around 0600, we walked outside: tree limbs and debris were everywhere, it was nature's way of creating a first-class mess. The storm allowed many of our tall trees to calve their limbs and large branches naturally; fortunately none fell on the roof. Surprisingly, there was not too much standing water—we didn't know it then but the real devastation of Erin was yet to come, in a few more hours—huge amounts of rain!

That morning at about 0700 Mary was to have left for Orlando International Airport to visit my Aunt Violet in Albany, Oregon. When we called the airline the day before to learn whether the flight was on or off because of the oncoming hurricane, the agent told us that the rescheduled flight might leave early in the afternoon of the second; we were surprised that the airport would reopen so soon. While we were preparing to leave for the airport, Erin's rain had started, but giving little hint to what was in store for Melbourne Village and area in the next few hours.

The trip to Orlando was uneventful. The airport was operating, with little evidence that it had been struck by a tropical storm a few hours earlier. Halfway back to Melbourne the rain began to increase. However, I took little notice. But on I-95 a few miles before the intersection with Highway 192 near West Melbourne, the downpour started. The rain was so heavy (the worst I have ever been in) that traffic came to a near halt; I could not see anything out of my windshield even with wipers moving full blast. I drove slowly with my head out the driver's window. It took an hour to move a distance that normally takes a few minutes.

As I approached the intersection with Highway 192 on I-95, the disaster of Erin's rain became evident. Except for a small portion of its inside lane, Highway 192 and shoulder were flooded as far as you could see. I knew if I stopped I would never get started again;

I also figured that the road would be closed very soon. Cars and pickups were stranded randomly on the shoulder. But I proceeded onto Highway 192 anyway, traveling that small open area of the inside lane. I made it all the way to the entrance to Melbourne Village. As I drove into the Village, its streets were likewise flooded. Water was everywhere but I just kept moving, keeping a light pedal on my brakes, trying to keep them as dry as possible (you can't stop a car with wet brakes). Fortunately I made it to my driveway, which was under a foot or so of water. In fact a "lake" surrounded our house (and many other houses in the Village); the log poles that normally border our driveway were floating all around the driveway. Later that afternoon Scott Taylor, my neighbor, took his family on a canoe ride, paddling up and down Village roads.

Several Village homes were flooded. Several days later after things begin to dry out, some residents put their ruined rugs and destroyed furniture and belongings on the curb for pickup by the garbage truck.

The greatest damage occurred at the Village entrance, where the Target department store stands. So much rain fell in such a short time that Target's roof caved in. The store was closed for several weeks for repair and restocking. Three days passed before the "lake" disappeared around our house. Melbourne Village residents were without power about five days.

By 6:00 P.M. Erin was 90 miles southeast of Apalachicola, moving west at 17 mph. At 6:00 A.M. on August 3, Erin was a hurricane again, 75 miles southeast of Pensacola. Winds were 80 mph and pressure was 28.79 inches. Erin peaked in this area, with 90 mph winds and lowest pressure of 28.74 inches, having become a strong Category 1 storm.

The second landfall was near Pensacola, but 90 mph winds were felt as far north as Jackson, Mississippi (fig. 16.D). On August 4, Erin was 30 miles northeast of Jackson, moving northwest at 10 mph. The storm still had 30 mph winds, and the last advisory was issued.

Caught by the storm during passage from the Bahamas to Florida, the 234-foot gambling-cruise ship *Club Royale* sank 90 miles east of Cape Canaveral, with loss of three crewmen. Six more people died in the Atlantic and Gulf of Mexico. Erin managed to dump heavy rains as far north as Illinois. The system finally died out in West Virginia after rain-ing on Alabama, Mississippi, Tennessee, Kentucky, Ohio, and Indiana.

More than 150,000 people were without electricity in east-central Florida for up to 10 days. Up to 12 inches of rain fell before any relief was felt. Damage was more than $700 million (fig. 16.E).

There was a reprieve of sorts as Tropical Depression 6 formed in the Bay of Campeche but did not develop further. Category 4 Felix, Tropical Storm Gabrielle, and Hurricanes Humberto and Iris, both Category 2, kept things interesting in August and September but did not leave the Atlantic. Tropical Depression 11 was brewing in the Florida Straits just north of the Cuban coast on August 22.

On August 23 at about 6:00 P.M., Jerry was named and was about to make landfall close to where Erin had struck (color plate 5). The system, a very wet tropical storm, took a track through Florida similar to Erin's (fig. 17). Top winds were 53 mph at Lake Worth and pressure was 29.59 inches. By 6:00 P.M. on August 24 Jerry was just off Florida's west coast near Cedar Key. Erratic movement during the night brought the storm inland again near Cross City as a depression. By noon on the twenty-fifth Jerry was on the Florida-Georgia border, moving north-northwest at 8 mph.

For the next five days the system wandered around the southeastern United States, finally tracking back across Florida as a disturbance, moving southwest. By the first of September it was gone in the Gulf of Mexico southwest of Cape Romano. More than 15 inches of rain fell in Florida, which was still saturated with water from Erin. Jerry caused six deaths and damage amounting to $21 million.

In the meantime, Tropical Storm Karen, Category 4 Luis, and Cat-egory 3 Marilyn were tearing up the West Indies, and Category 1 Noel never quite made it into the Caribbean. This brought to an end a very active July and August, and only two storms, Luis and Marilyn, inhab-ited the usually active September.

Opal, September 27–October 5

Tropical Depression 14 fizzled out in the mid-Atlantic, but on Septem-ber 27, Tropical Depression 17 was discovered about 75 miles south-southwest of Cozumel in the northwest Caribbean. (Allison had started in the same general area.) By noon on September 28 the system was inland in Yucatan, and it drifted across the area until the thirtieth (fig. 18.A).

By noon on September 30 the system was over water and had intensified enough to be named—Opal, the first letter O storm since hurricane naming began in 1953. For the next day it drifted in a westerly direction in the warm waters of the Bay of Campeche. About 575 miles south-southwest of the mouth of the Mississippi River, Opal was stationary and became a hurricane, with 80 mph winds and pressure of 28.67 inches (color plate 6).

Early on October 3 the storm was moving north at 8 mph with barometric pressure dropping. Hurricane force winds were recorded 30 miles out and tropical storm winds to 275 miles in all directions. In less than 24 hours, Opal went from a Category 1 storm to Category 4, and early on the fourth the air reconnaissance flight clocked 148 mph sustained winds, with gusts to 185 mph. Pressure was Category 5 at 27.05 inches. This was the peak of Opal, which was now some 180 miles south of the Mississippi's mouth.

Opal had followed a path of water of 86°F and warmer through the Gulf of Mexico, which was the fuel needed to spawn a Category 4 or 5 hurricane. But an area of cooler water blocked its track to the Florida coast late on October 4. Opal made landfall between Destin and Panama City as a Category 3 storm (color plate 7). Sustained winds were 125 mph with gusts to 144; the storm surge was as high as 15 feet in places. This surge was evident along the coast from southeast Alabama down to Cedar Key, Florida. There was significant damage as far north as Atlanta, and the system finally died around the Great Lakes. Fifty-nine deaths had resulted: 9 in the United States, 31 in Guatemala, and 19 in Mexico. Damages exceeded $3 billion (fig. 18.B–E).

The season was not over by any means. Tropical Storms Pablo and Sebastien flared up in the Atlantic, and Roxanne, a Category 3 hurricane, threatened to follow Opal in the Gulf. There were anxious moments for Florida's Opal victims as Roxanne danced in the Bay of Campeche less than a week after Opal's impact. Tanya finally ended the season as an October–November Category 1 storm in the Atlantic. At one time near the end of August, Humberto, Iris, Karen, Jerry, and Luis were all going at once in the Atlantic (fig. 19)—just another Atlantic record set during the 1995 hurricane season.

5

The Hurricane Seasons of 1996 and 1997

The 1996 Season

Dr. William Gray of Colorado State University predicted 11 named storms for the 1996 hurricane season; seven would become hurricanes, and three of those would be major storms (Category 3, 4, or 5 on the Saffir-Simpson Scale), according to his projections. In fact there were 13 named storms, nine of which became hurricanes, and six of those were major storms (two Category 4 and four Category 3). The number of major storms is unusual: on average there are two per season. There have been only four other years when as many as six major storms occurred during the season.

Florida had one direct hit and two close calls, yet seven storms threatened the state. A disturbance in May, moving from south-southwest to northeast across the state produced a lot of rain and attention from the National Hurricane Center. After the disturbance came the threat from Bertha, in July, which came within 200 miles of Florida's north coast. Edouard headed for the Sunshine State but turned north, well away from the coast. Fran brought out warnings for the Bahamas, Florida, and the coast north to the Carolinas before indeed curving north to hit the Carolinas.

Tropical Storm Josephine started as Tropical Depression 10 in the southwest Gulf of Mexico on October 4. The track was basically northeast to a landfall in the Florida Panhandle on the evening of October 7. Winds of 65 mph and a storm surge of 6–9 feet occurred in the Florida Big Bend area just east of St. Marks. Nine tornadoes were reported across the state, and 131 mobile homes were damaged, two dozen of them seriously in Putnam County, south of Jacksonville. Only three injuries were reported, a welcome low; for a short time 100,000 households were without electricity. Damage estimated at $400,000 in Florida resulted from tornadoes alone. Sixteen counties opened 36 shelters to about 1,900 people. Jacksonville got the most rain, nearly 13 inches. Lowest barometric pressure measured was 28.97 inches, and peak winds hit 70 mph. Color plate 8 shows the storm approaching Florida.

Also in October, Hurricane Lili (color plate 9) started in the northwest Caribbean as Tropical Depression 12, beginning in the same area as Allison, Opal, and Roxanne in 1995. Original model forecasts tracked the storm across western Cuba and then to Florida's west-central coast. But by October 16, the track was moving east through the Florida Straits, the center of the storm missing Florida altogether. An approaching cold front saved the day. On the seventeenth, tropical storm warnings were hoisted for the Florida Keys, and the warnings remained through the eighteenth. Lili made landfall on the southern Cuban coast, but rain bands and tropical storm winds impacted Florida as far north as Cape Canaveral. The storm's east-northeast track eventually took it deep into the North Atlantic and Europe, after much damage was sustained in Cuba and the Bahamas.

Marco ended the 1996 season as an erratic Category 1 hurricane in the Caribbean in November. The processes of El Niño had produced the warming waters off the west coast of South America that led to heavy convection. These systems then move eastward and tend to inhibit tropical cyclone formation in the Atlantic Basin. The reverse is largely the case with La Niña, which enhances activity.

The 1997 Season

The four most active years on record for tropical cyclone activity in the Atlantic Basin were 1995 through 1998. The obvious intrusion of El Niño during the 1997 season had little effect on the overall four-year record but did leave 1997 a weaker than normal season. Only seven named storms got on record in 1997. Four were tropical storms, one was a Category 3 hurricane, and two were Category 1 hurricanes.

On July 16, Tropical Depression 4 in the Gulf of Mexico developed into a tropical storm and was named Danny. It became a slow-moving Category 1 hurricane, making landfall near the mouth of the Mississippi River on July 18. Another landfall occurred just southeast of Mobile, Alabama, on the nineteenth. The major effect from Danny was more than 40 inches of rainfall along most of its track with resulting significant inland flooding. The GOES 8 satellite image (color plates 10 and 11) shows Hurricane Danny at near peak intensity with outflow over most of the Florida Panhandle and North Florida.

Hurricane warnings were issued eastward as far as Destin in Florida as Danny's rain bands moved over the central and northern parts of the state. Later that day, the storm took a jog to the east, a somewhat rare move for a Gulf storm in July. This brought out warnings eastward to Apalachicola.

Late on July 19, tropical storm warnings were flying over Panama City, Florida. The storm caused freshwater flooding inland. Bay County had over 8 inches of rain and Pensacola 6.78 inches. Tides in Walton County were over 2 feet.

However, shortly after the second landfall, Danny was downgraded to a tropical storm, then to a depression, and it proceeded to move slowly over the southeastern United States for the next four days. While rather weak, it was nevertheless well defined on satellite images. Peak intensity on July 18 resulted in 101 mph wind speed and a low pressure of 29.05 inches. Four people were killed by the storm, and total damage was over $100 million.

There were no August tropical storms or hurricanes for the first time in 36 years.

6

The Hurricane Season of 1998

The year 1998 produced 14 named storms, one more than 1996 but just a few short of the near-record 19 of the 1995 season. There had been four tropical storms, three Category 1 hurricanes, four Category 2 hurricanes, and one each Category 3, 4, and 5. The last, Mitch, was only the sixth category 5 hurricane in the Atlantic Basin in the twentieth century. The 1998 hurricane season did not suffer from the El Niño syndrome like 1997 did. El Niño was long gone, and La Niña was firmly in place.

One can clearly see the different effects that El Niño and La Niña have on Atlantic tropical cyclone activity: three of the 1998 storms tracked across Florida, two as tropical storms and one as a hurricane.

Earl (August 31–September 3) was the first Florida tropical storm since Josephine in 1996 and struck basically the same area, the Florida Panhandle. At noon on September 2, Earl was 140 miles southwest of Destin and rated close to being a Category 2 hurricane, bypassing the tropical depression category. Reported winds were 100 mph, with 29.23 inches of barometric pressure, and the storm was stationary. By 6:00 P.M. that day, Hurricane Earl was predicted to make landfall near Panama City. Winds were measured at 90 mph and pressure had fallen to 29.11 inches. The hurricane was now moving northeast at 10 mph, accompanied by heavy rains with winds of tropical storm force out almost 200 miles in all directions.

On the third at 6:00 A.M., Earl was 40 miles north-northeast of Panama City, moving northeast at 10–15 mph. Winds were 75 mph and pressure 29.11 inches. Tropical storm winds were 200 miles to the southeast, and hurricane force winds were about 115 miles to the east and southeast. Color plate 12 is a satellite image of the storm late on

September 2, just before landfall near Panama City. Three deaths were attributed to the storm, and the total damage was $80 million.

The second Florida storm was Hurricane Georges (pronounced *johrj*, as in French, although it often seemed to come out sounding like the standard English George). Georges (September 15–29) started as Tropical Depression 7 and was a Cape Verde storm that tracked westward perfectly through the Atlantic. It also managed to cross every landmass in the Caribbean Sea, not characteristic of hurricanes. Even though the storm spent much time over some form of land, it managed to maintain its hurricane status. Its first landfall was Antigua, followed by Puerto Rico, the Dominican Republic, Cuba, Florida, and then Mississippi.

It was decided to evacuate all but essential personnel from the Key West and adjoining naval facilities, and action was taken early. The result was a well-organized progression along the single 149-mile way out, Highway 1. By September 24, most of the Key West facilities were boarded up and ready for the impact of Georges.

At 8:00 that evening, Georges was about 200 miles southeast of Key West, moving west-northwest at 14 mph. Pressure was 29.12 inches and winds over 85 mph. Hurricane force winds were out 35 miles in all directions, and tropical storm force winds covered 175 miles.

Early on September 25, Georges was in the Florida Straits, and by noon it was pounding Key West. Peak winds were 105 to 110 mph (Category 2), and the barometer was down to 28.79 inches. Heavy rains and tides resulted in heavy damage in the Keys. The most severe damage was in the middle Keys, where boats were grounded, homes were flooded, and walls were blown out. The surge was estimated to be over 6 feet from watermarks on some dwellings. The runways at Boca Chica Naval Air Station were 10–16 inches underwater. But not a soul was lost, proving once again that evacuation planning and execution are vital—the safest place to be in a hurricane is to not be there in the first place.

By 6:00 P.M. on the twenty-fifth, Georges was 75 miles west-northwest of Key West but still in the Keys, with winds to 105 mph on that west-northwest track at 14 mph. Color plate 13 shows Hurricane Georges at about noon on September 25 at Key West. The back cover of this book shows Hurricane Georges three hours later. The Atlantic was busy that day, with Georges in the Florida Straits, Tropical Storm Karl near 30.0N and 53.0W, Hurricane Ivan near 35.0N and 42.0W, and Hurricane Jeanne near 20.0N and 39.0W (color plate 14). Color plate 15 is a montage of the track of Hurricane Georges. Typical Category 1 damage in Key West and Category 3 damage in the Big Pine Key area are shown in figure 20.A–B. Georges killed more than 600 people in the Caribbean, but only one was killed in the United States. Total U.S. damage was estimated at $5.91 billion.

The saga of Hurricane Mitch was another story. This system was tracked across the Atlantic from the Cape Verde Islands and became erratic in the southwest Caribbean Sea near 12.0N and 77.0W October 21–23. The newly named Tropical Storm Mitch finally moved to the northeast on October 24, but by the next morning it was back on a westward heading as a full hurricane.

The next eight days produced a Category 5 hurricane with a devastating track through Honduras, Nicaragua, El Salvador, Guatemala, Belize, and northward through Yucatan. The last death count was close to 11,000 people. On November 4, Mitch had emerged from the Yucatan into the Gulf of Mexico as a tropical depression, heading northeast. Once the system was in the Gulf, it did not take long to regain tropical storm status, and the track was toward Florida.

Florida landfall was near Naples with sustained winds of 65 mph and pressure of 29.23 inches. Mitch was moving east-northeast at 26 mph. It made its exit into the Atlantic Ocean just north of Jupiter at about 10:00 A.M. on November 5. Color plate 16 shows Tropical Storm Mitch approaching Florida, and color plate 17 shows Mitch crossing south-central Florida on the way into the Atlantic. Estimated U.S. damage was about $40 million, mostly from tornadoes in the Florida Keys.

Florida has been stuck by only one Category 5 hurricane, the Great Labor Day Hurricane of September 2, 1935.

7

The Hurricane Season of 1999

There were 12 named storms in the 1999 season. Four were tropical storms, eight were hurricanes, and five of those were intense hurricanes (Category 3, 4, or 5 on the Saffir-Simpson Scale). All five of the intense storms were Category 4, which was a record in the Atlantic Basin. The remaining three hurricanes were Category 2. The years 1995, 1996, 1997, 1998, and 1999 were the five most active seasons in a row ever recorded in the Atlantic Basin.

Four storms affected Florida: three were hurricanes and one a weak tropical storm. The first threat to Florida in 1999 was Dennis (August 24–September 7), a Category 2 storm (color plate 18). A hurricane watch was posted along the Florida east coast on August 27 and 28, but the storm curved more to the north and missed the Florida east coast by about 115 miles off Melbourne (color plate 19). Winds were 105 mph and the barometer 28.61 inches. The diameter of hurricane force winds was about 85 miles, and tropical storm force winds were out some 175 miles. Heavy surf was the main Florida coastal problem, and some erosion occurred, as is typical for a system paralleling the coast. The total damage was $157 million and there were four deaths in Florida caused by high surf.

Floyd (September 7–17) was a Category 4 storm, the most powerful of the year. It caused the evacuation of nearly 2 million people, mostly in Florida—possibly the largest evacuation in U.S. history. Floyd made no landfall in Florida, but the effects were felt on the state's whole east coast. Warnings were posted September 12 and 13 as Floyd plodded northwest, then north, then northwest again (color plate 20). The center ran about 100 miles to the east, but the storm was 600 miles in diameter. The radius of maximum winds was more than 60 miles (color plate 21).

There was literally no room at the inn as evacuation proceeded. Motels and hotels filled up fast, and vehicles were bumper to bumper on highways in too many cases; this was apparent all the way over to the west coast of Florida. There were accounts of some people going as far as Nebraska and Michigan. Tropical storm force winds and very high surf did most of the damage in Florida. Once again, the state was lucky, as a cold front running northeast-southwest across the Jacksonville area kept the storm off the Florida coast. The NOAA weather buoy, about 140 miles east of Port Canaveral, recorded 58-foot seas, 155 mph winds, and barometric pressure of 27.16 inches—figures that place Floyd right at a Category 5 hurricane status.

Tropical Storm Harvey (September 19–22) was a Gulf storm heading for the Tampa area when an abrupt turn to the southeast caused a weak landfall near Naples. Winds were about 50 mph at landfall and soon afterward a frontal system absorbed Harvey on September 22, just east of the Miami area (color plate 22). Damage was nevertheless about $15 million. No deaths or injuries were good news, but there was plenty of rain in South Florida.

Hurricane Irene (October 13–19), a Category 2 storm, kept people's adrenaline flowing because of its erratic track. It began in the southwestern Caribbean on October 13. The storm moved north across western Cuba, becoming a hurricane in the Florida Straits on the fourteenth (color plate 23). Models indicated that the track would be into the Gulf, but Irene later changed direction to go up the west coast of Florida (color plate 24).

On October 15, it was across South Florida in the Flamingo area, delivering 10–20 inches of rain. Freshwater flooding occurred in many areas. Winds of 103 mph were recorded at Big Pine Key on the fifteenth. At about 6:00 P.M. that day, Irene was 45 miles west-southwest of Miami with 85 mph winds, moving north-northeast at 10 mph. Early in the morning of October 16, the storm managed to do some major roof damage to John Williams's home in Palm Bay. Gusts were over 80 mph and sustained winds about 60–70 mph; the winds lasted for more than four hours. The system moved into the Atlantic Ocean just east of Melbourne and headed for the North Carolina coast (color plate 25). In Florida eight people were electrocuted or drowned, and the damage was $800 million.

8

The Hurricane Seasons of 2000 and 2001

The 2000 Season

Although the 2000 season had only a minimal impact on Florida, it was a busy one. There were 14 named storms: eight became hurricanes, and there were six tropical storms (Franklin and Avila 2001). Two of the hurricanes were Category 4 storms, one was Category 2, and the rest were Category 1. There were 54 deaths in the United States, and damage was $27 million (not high for an average season). This does not include the $950 million in damage done by the "precursor disturbance" of the system that became Tropical Storm Leslie. (Precursor disturbance is a name coined by the National Hurricane Center; it is applied only to the system that ran ahead of the actual named storm and caused all the damage.) Three of the storms mentioned struck the coast of Florida, causing four deaths. Three people died in the Leslie system, and one died near Pensacola while surfing during Gordon.

Hurricane Gordon (September 14–18), a Category 1 hurricane, was the first of the season to make landfall in Florida, striking near Cedar Key, close to the mouth of the Suwannee River as a strong tropical storm. Winds were down to 70 mph on the evening of September 17, and the barometer read 29.26 inches. Tropical storm winds were as far out as 105 miles in all directions. Several tornadoes were reported in central and south Florida. The damage in the United States, including Florida, was estimated to be $11 million.

Tropical Storm Helene (September 15–25) made landfall near Fort Walton Beach the morning of September 22 (color plate 26; the

Fujawhara effect is the counteraction sometimes evident when two systems are in close proximity to each other). Maximum sustained winds were near 40 mph, and the barometer was 29.61 inches. Flooding was reported to be heavy in the Florida Panhandle and Georgia. Tallahassee received 8–10 inches of rain. There were no deaths in Florida during Helene's passage, and damage was about $16 million in the United States, including Florida. The last advisory on Helene was issued just southeast of Columbus, Georgia, later that day.

Tropical Storm Leslie (October 4–7) was a unique system in that as a precursor disturbance, it caused the most damage and deaths in Florida of any system in 2000. A stationary band of heavy rainfall developed across southeastern Florida, resulting in 12- to 18-inch accumulations (color plate 27). The heavy rain generated flood damage estimated at $950 million. By October 4 a well-defined circulation developed east of Orlando and moved into the Atlantic Ocean. Leslie became a subtropical depression but was not a full tropical storm until east of St. Augustine, out in the Atlantic (color plate 28). The original system started as a low in the Florida Straits, near Dry Tortugas, on October 2. Highest winds were a little more than 35–40 mph, and the lowest pressure reading was 29.85 inches near Daytona Beach.

There were no hurricane landfalls in the United States in the 2000 season, an occurrence that has happened only 13 times in 50 years.

The 2001 Season

The 2001 hurricane season was similar to that of 2000 in that both had above normal activity but minimal impact on the state of Florida.

Dr. William Gray, Colorado State University, predicted there would be 12 named storms in 2001: seven would become hurricanes and three major storms (3, 4, and 5 on the Saffir-Simpson Scale). The year ended with 15 named storms, 9 hurricanes, and 4 major storms (color plate 32).

The first to affect Florida was Tropical Storm Allison (June 4–6). It actually started as a tropical wave from Africa that tracked across the Atlantic, into the Caribbean and Gulf of Mexico where it became TD-1. The system made landfall near Galveston, Texas, as a tropical storm on

June 5. By June 11, two tornadoes were spotted in Madison County, Florida, and a third near Tallahassee from the eastward-moving remnants of Allison. Rain bands from Allison stalled near Tallahassee. More than ten inches of rain fell just west of the capital, and Tallahassee recorded a total of 9.86 inches on June 11 and 12. Rain continued across North Florida as the remnants of Allison drifted east through June 12 and 13.

From June 10 to the last of July there was little activity in the Atlantic, possibly due to excessive Saharan dust. This sometimes can cause sea surface temperatures to become cooler, thus inhibiting tropical cyclone development.

The system that became Tropical Storm Barry (August 1–6) was tracked from an African wave into the Gulf of Mexico, where it became TD-3 on the first of August. Barry moved erratically west, then back to the east, then finally tracked north to a landfall just to the west of Panama City, Florida, with winds more than 65 mph late on August 5 (color plate 29). Tides were 2–4 feet above normal, and 6–8 inches of rain fell in the track area. Eglin Air Force Base reported a wind gust to 63 mph; pressure was 29.44 inches. The forward speed of Barry was only 9 mph.

On September 11, TD-8 formed near 25.0N–85.W in the Gulf of Mexico. Late on September 13, Tropical Storm Gabrielle (September 11–18) was named and tracked north-northeast toward Florida's west coast (color plate 30). The center came ashore about 8:00 A.M. on September 14 near Venice. Sarasota's downtown area was flooded, schools were shut down, tornadoes knocked over trees and power lines, and 5–10 inches of rain fell in the area. About 160,000 homes and businesses were left without power in Florida. A motel roof in Bradenton was blown off. More than 100 mobile home residents had taken shelter there. Tornadoes were spotted in Brevard, Volusia, and Charlotte counties, and Gabrielle pushed the Peace River into the town of Punta Gorda, flooding downtown streets with 3 feet of water. On September 15, the storm finally broke into the Atlantic Ocean near Cape Canaveral and accelerated northeast. Some 700 miles east of Cape Hatteras it briefly became a hurricane, then died two days later about 800 miles east of the New England area.

Hurricane Michelle (October 29–November 7) was another story— one of those "Boy, are we Floridians lucky that it missed us!" And lucky we were. Michelle's track was similar to Lili's in 1996 in that they both started in the northwestern Caribbean and tracked northward toward Cuba and Florida. The northward movement continued and caused evacuation in the Florida Keys on November 4. Michelle was near a Cuban landfall at this point with gusts to 155 mph and seas 12–14 feet (a Category 4 storm) moving only 5 mph. Landfall occurred about 6:00 P.M. on November 4 near the famous Bay of Pigs site (color plate 31). After that, the hoped-for turn toward the east occurred, and there was no Florida landfall. Michelle moved east-northeast rapidly, losing tropical characteristics and finally dying about 300 miles south of Bermuda on November 7.

To conclude, the tracks of the 2001 season are shown in color plate 32. As of December 2001, details of the dollar damage, casualties, and other storm-related facts were not available on the 2001 storms. Jack Beven's article in *Weatherwise* magazine (March/April 2002) gives the best details on the 2001 Atlantic hurricane season. According the Beven, "Allison was the deadliest and costliest U.S. Tropical Storm on record . . . more than $5 billion in damages . . . 41 deaths." Eight of the deaths occurred in Florida.

Appendix 1. Hurricane Preparedness

Be Prepared Before the Hurricane Season

- Know the storm surge history and elevation of your area.
- Learn safe routes inland.
- Learn locations of official shelters.
- Review needs and working condition of emergency equipment such as flashlights and battery-powered radios.
- Ensure that nonperishable food and water supplies on hand are sufficient to last for at least two weeks.
- Obtain and store the materials necessary to secure your home properly, such as plywood and plastic.
- Check your home for loose and clogged rain gutters and downspouts.
- Keep trees and shrubbery trimmed. Cut weak branches and trees that could fall or bump against the house. When trimming, try to create a channel through the foliage to the center of the tree to allow for air flow.
- Determine where to move your boat in an emergency.
- Review your insurance policy to ensure that it provides adequate coverage.
- Individuals with special needs should contact the local Office of Emergency Management.
- For information and assistance with any of these items, contact your local National Weather Service office, Office of Emergency Management, or American Red Cross chapter.

When a Hurricane Watch Is Issued

- Monitor radio, television, NOAA Weather Radio, or hurricane hotline telephone numbers frequently for official bulletins of the storm's progress.
- Fuel and service family vehicles.
- Inspect and secure mobile home tie-downs.
- Prepare to cover all window and door openings with shutters or other shielding materials.

Check Food and Water Supplies

- Have clean, airtight containers on hand to store at least a two-week supply of drinking water (14 gallons per person).
- Stock up on canned provisions.
- Get a camping stove with fuel.
- Keep a small cooler with frozen gel packs handy for packing refrigerated items.
- Check prescription medicines; obtain at least ten days' to two weeks' supply.
- Stock up on extra batteries for radios, flashlights, and lanterns.
- Prepare to store and secure outdoor lawn furniture and other loose, lightweight objects, such as garbage cans, garden tools, and potted plants.
- Check and replenish first aid supplies.
- Have an extra supply of cash on hand.

When a Hurricane Warning Is Issued

- Closely monitor radio, TV, NOAA Weather Radio, or hurricane hotline telephone numbers for official bulletins.
- Follow instructions issued by local officials. Leave immediately if ordered to do so.

- Complete preparation activities, such as putting up storm shutters and securing loose objects.
- Evacuate areas that might be affected by storm surge flooding.
- If evacuating, leave early (if possible, in daylight).
- Leave mobile homes in any case.
- Notify neighbors and a family member outside the warned area of your evacuation plans.

Evacuation

Plan to evacuate if you:

- live in a mobile home. Do not stay in a mobile home under any circumstances. They are unsafe in high wind and/or hurricane conditions, no matter how well fastened to the ground;
- live on the coastline, on an island, near a river, or in a flood plain;
- live in a high-rise. Hurricane winds are stronger at higher elevations. Glass doors and windows may be blown out of their casings and weaken the structure.

When you leave:

- Stay with friends or relatives or at low-rise inland hotels or motels outside the flood zones.
- Leave early to avoid heavy traffic, roads blocked by early flood waters, and bridges impassable due to high winds.
- Put food and water out for pets if you cannot take them with you. Public shelters do not allow pets, and nor do most motels/hotels.
- Go to a hurricane shelter if you have no other place to go. Shelters may be crowded and uncomfortable, with no privacy and no electricity. Do not leave your home for a shelter until government officials announce on radio or TV that a particular shelter is open.

What to bring to a shelter:

- first aid kit; medicine; baby food and diapers; cards, games, and books; toiletries; battery-powered radio; flashlight (one per person); extra batteries; blankets or sleeping bags; identification, valuable papers (insurance), and cash.

If Staying at Home

- Reminder: Only stay on in a home if you have not been ordered to leave. If you *are* told to leave, do so immediately!
- Store water. Fill sterilized jugs and bottles with water for a two-week supply of drinking water. Fill bathtub and large containers with water for sanitary purposes.
- Turn refrigerator to maximum cold, and open it only when necessary.
- Turn off utilities if told to do so by authorities. Turn off propane tanks.
- Unplug small appliances.
- Stay inside a well-constructed building. Examine the building and plan in advance what you will do if winds become strong. Strong winds can produce deadly missiles and structural failure.

If winds grow strong:

- Stay away from windows and doors, even if they are covered. Take refuge in a small interior room, closet, or hallway. Take a battery-powered radio, a NOAA Weather Radio, and flashlight with you to your place of refuge.
- Close all interior doors. Secure and brace external doors, particularly double inward-opening doors and garage doors.
- If you are in a two-story house, go to the basement, an interior first-floor room such as a bathroom or closet, or under the stairs.
- If you are in a multistory building and away from the water, go to the first or second floor and take refuge in a hall or interior room, away

from windows. Interior stairwells and the areas around elevator shafts are generally the strongest part of a building.

- Lie on the floor under a table or another sturdy object.
- Be alert for tornadoes, which often are spawned by hurricanes.
- **If the "eye" of the hurricane should pass over your area, be aware that the improved weather conditions are temporary. The storm conditions will return with winds coming from the opposite direction, sometimes within just a few minutes and usually within an hour.**

After the Storm Passes

- Stay in your protected area until announcements are made on the radio or TV that the dangerous winds have passed.
- If you have evacuated, do not return home until officials announce that your area is ready. Remember, proof of residency may be required in order to reenter evacuated zones.
- If your home or building has structural damage, do not enter until it is checked by officials.
- Avoid using candles and other open flames indoors.
- Beware of outdoor hazards.
- Avoid downed power lines and any water in which they may be lying. Be alert for poisonous snakes, often driven from their dens by high water. Beware of weakened bridges and washed-out roads. Watch for weakened limbs on trees and/or damaged overhanging structures.
- Do not use the telephone unless absolutely necessary. The system usually is jammed with calls during and after a hurricane.
- Guard against spoiled food. Use dry or canned food. Do not drink or prepare food with tap water until you are certain it is not contaminated.
- When cutting up fallen trees, use caution, especially if you use a chain saw. Serious injuries can occur when these powerful machines snap back or when the chain breaks.

Source: NOAA, 1993.

Appendix 2. Glossary

EST: Eastern Standard Time.

Flash flood warning: A flash flood has been reported or is imminent—take immediate action.

Flash flood watch: Flash flood conditions are possible within the designated watch area, so be alert.

Fujawhara effect: The effect produced when two systems are in close proximity to each other.

GMT: Greenwich Mean Time.

GOES: Geostationary Orbiting Environmental Satellite.

Hurricane: A tropical cyclone in which maximum sustained surface wind is 74 mph (64 knots) or greater.

Hurricane warning: A warning that sustained winds of 74 mph (64 knots) or higher are expected in a specified coastal area within 24 hours or less.

Hurricane watch: An announcement that hurricane conditions pose a possible threat to a specified coastal area within 36 hours.

IR: Infrared radiation.

NOAA: National Oceanic and Atmospheric Administration.

Small craft advisories: When a tropical cyclone threatens a coastal area, small craft operators are advised to remain in port or not to venture into the open sea.

Storm surge: An abnormal rise of the sea along a shore, primarily as a result of the winds of a storm.

Tropical cyclone: By international agreement, this is the general term for all cyclone circulations originating over tropical waters, classified by form and intensity.

Tropical depression: A tropical cyclone in which the maximum sustained surface wind is 38 mph (33 knots) or less.

Tropical disturbance: A moving area of thunderstorms in the tropics that maintains its identity for 24 hours or more; a common phenomenon in the tropics.

Tropical storm: A tropical cyclone in which the maximum sustained surface wind ranges from 39 to 73 mph (34–63 knots) inclusive.

Tropical storm warning: A warning for tropical storm conditions, including sustained winds within the range of 39 to 73 mph (34–63 knots), expected in a specified coastal area within 24 hours or less.

Tropical storm watch: Used for a coastal area when there is the threat of tropical storm conditions within 36 hours.

Tropical wave: A trough of low pressure in the trade-wind easterlies.

References

Anon. 1926. Tropical Hurricane Spreads Disasters along East Coast. *Melbourne* (Fla.) *Journal*, July 27, 1926.

Anon. 1928. Northern Extremity of Tropical Hurricane Sweeps through Melbourne. *Melbourne* (Fla.) *Times-Journal*, August 10, 1928.

Antonini, G. A., P. W. Box, E. Brady, M. Clarke, H. R. Ledesma, and J. L. Rahn. 1993. *Location and Assessment of Hurricane Andrew Damaged Vessels on Biscayne Bay and Adjoining Shores*. Gainesville: Florida Sea Grant College Program. 58 pp.

Avila, L. A., and R. J. Pasch. 1997. Atlantic Hurricane Season. *Weatherwise* 50, no. 1 (February/March): 36–40.

Beven, J. 2002. Atlantic Hurricanes. *Weatherwise* 55, no. 1 (March/April): 32–39.

Bigelow, F. H. 1898. Features of Hurricanes. In *Yearbook of the Department of Agriculture* (for 1898). Quoted in E. B. Garriott, *West Indian Hurricanes*. Washington, D.C.: Weather Bureau. 69 pp. and tracking charts.

Clark, R. C. 1986a. *The Impact of Hurricane Elena and TS Juan on Coastal Construction in Florida*. Beaches and Shores Post-Storm Report 85-3. Tallahassee: Department of Natural Resources, Division of Beaches and Shores, State of Florida. 142 pp.

———. 1986b. *Hurricane Kate*. Beaches and Shores Post-Storm Report 86-1. Tallahassee: Department of Natural Resources, Division of Beaches and Shores, State of Florida. 114 pp.

Dunn, G. E., and B. I. Miller. 1964. *Atlantic Hurricanes*. Baton Rouge: Louisiana State University Press. 377 pp.

Dunn, G. E., and Staff. 1967. *Florida Hurricanes*. Technical Memorandum WBTM SR-38. Coral Gables: Environmental Sciences Services Administration, National Hurricane Center.

Frank, N. 1978. Hurricanes in Brevard County. *Florida Today* (Melbourne), June 4.

Franklin, J., and L. Avila. 2001. Atlantic Hurricanes. *Weatherwise* 54, no. 2 (March/April): 28–33.

Garriott, E. B. 1900. *West Indian Hurricanes*. Washington, D.C.: Weather Bureau.

Goldenberg, S. B., C. W. Landsea, A. B. Mestas-Nunez, and W. M. Gray. 2001. The Recent Increase in Atlantic Hurricane Activity: Causes and Implications. *Science* 293: 381–560.

Gray, W. M. 1990. Strong Association between West African Rainfall and U.S. Landfall of Intense Hurricanes. *Science* 249: 1251–56.

Hebert, P. J., J. D. Jarrell, and M. Mayfield. 1997. *The Deadliest, Costliest, and Most Intense United States Hurricanes of This Century (and Other Frequently Requested Hurricane Facts)*. NOAA Technical Memorandum NWS TPC-1. Miami: National Oceanic and Atmospheric Administration, National Weather Service, National Hurricane Center. 40 pp.

Holmes, G. W. 1876. Letter to a friend. F. A. Hopwood personal collection, Melbourne, Fla., 1985.

Lawrence, Lucia. 1926. Letter belonging to Ruth Warner, September–October 2. Copies in possession of authors.

Lawrence, M., L. Avila, J. Beven, J. Franklin, J. Guiney, and R. Pasch. 2000. Atlantic Hurricanes. *Weatherwise* 53, no. 2 (March/April): 39–43.

National Climatic Center. 1954–79. *North Atlantic Tropical Cyclones Series (1954–1979)*. Climatological Data, National Summary Volumes. Asheville, N.C.: National Climatic Center. Each year paginated.

National Oceanic and Atmospheric Administration (NOAA). 1970–79. Climatological Data, National Summary, vols. 21–30, no. 13. Asheville, N.C.: National Climatic Center. Unpaginated.

———. 1982. *Some Devastating North Atlantic Hurricanes of the 20th Century*. U.S. Department of Commerce, NOAA, Stock no. 003-017-00401-5. Washington, D.C.: U.S. Government Printing Office. 14 pp.

———. 1999. *Tropical Cyclones of the North Atlantic Ocean, 1871–1986*. Historical Climatology Series 6-2. Asheville, N.C.: National Climatic Center. 206 pp.

———. 1993. *Hurricanes: A Familiarization Booklet*. Rev. April 1983. NOAA PA 91001. Coral Gables, Fla.: National Oceanic and Atmospheric Administration, National Hurricane Center. 36 pp.

Norton, G. 1949. *Florida Hurricanes*. Rev. ed. U.S. Weather Bureau Publication, Washington, D.C. 6 pp. (Originally Florida Hurricanes by R. W. Gray, *Monthly Weather Review* 61, no. 1 [January 1933].)

Pasch, R. J. 1999. Atlantic Hurricanes. *Weatherwise* 52, no. 2 (March/April): 48–53.

Rabac, G. 1986. *The City of Cocoa Beach: The First Sixty Years*. Winona, Minn.: Apollo Books.

Rappaport, E. N. 1998. Atlantic Hurricanes. *Weatherwise* 51, no. 2 (March/April): 43–46.

Simpson, R. H., and H. Riehl. 1981. *The Hurricane and Its Impact*. Baton Rouge: Louisiana State University Press. 399 pp.

Sugg, A. L. 1966. The Hurricane Season of 1965. *Monthly Weather Review* 94, no. 3: 183–91.

Sugg, A. L., L. G. Pardue, and R. L. Carrodus. 1971. *Memorable Hurricanes of the United States since 1873*. NOAA Technical Memorandum NWS SR-56. Fort Worth, Tex.: National Oceanic and Atmospheric Administration, National Weather Service, Southern Region. 52 pp.

Tannehill, I. R. 1938. *Hurricanes: Their Nature and History*. Princeton, N.J.: Princeton University Press. 304 pp.

U.S. Army Corps of Engineers. 1993. *Hurricane Andrew Storm Summary and Impacts on the Beaches of Florida*. Special Report. Jacksonville District, Fla.: U.S. Army Corps of Engineers. 61 pp. and appendices.

U.S. Weather Bureau, Monthly and Annual Reports. 1897–1965. Climatological Data, Florida, April 1897–December 1965. National Climatic Center, Asheville, N.C. Microfiche 112.

Yanaros, J. 1986. Damage Caused by Hurricane in Ft. Pierce, 1933. Personal communication, Melbourne, Fla.

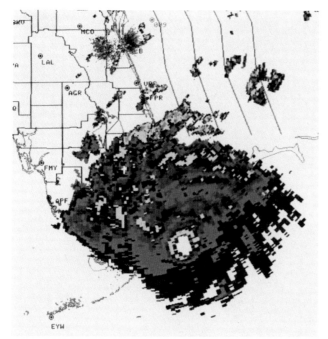

Plate 1. Doppler radar of Hurricane Andrew, 1992. This Doppler is from the National Weather Service office in Melbourne, Florida, recorded after Miami's radar was blown away. This image was taken at an extreme range of 160 nautical miles. (Courtesy of the National Weather Service, Melbourne Office)

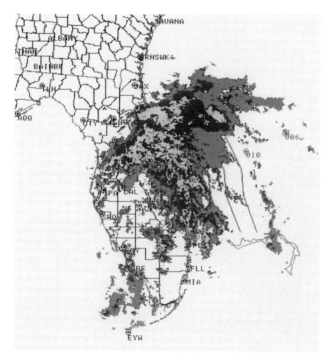

Plate 2. Doppler Radar of Hurricane Gordon, Florida landfall, 1994. (Courtesy of the National Weather Service, Melbourne Office)

Plate 3. Satellite photograph, Hurricane Allison. (Courtesy of Mike Witiw)

Plate 4. Doppler radar, Hurricane Erin landfall, Florida, 1995. (Courtesy of the National Weather Service, Melbourne Office)

Left: Plate 5. Tropical Storm Jerry, radar, 1995. (Courtesy of the National Weather Service, Melbourne Office)

Below: Plate 6. Satellite photograph, Hurricane Opal, Category 4 hurricane at 1315 on October 4, 1995. (Courtesy of Mike Witiw)

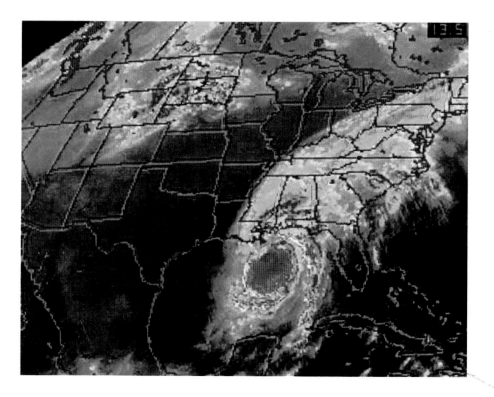

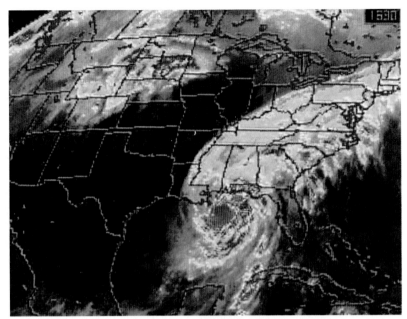

Plate 7. Satellite photograph, Hurricane Opal, Category 4 hurricane at 1630 on October 4, 1995. (Courtesy of Mike Witiw)

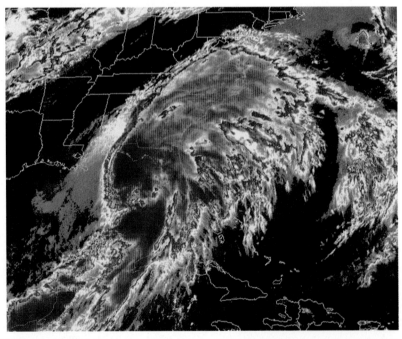

Plate 8. Tropical Storm Josephine approaches the Florida coast on October 7, 1996. (Courtesy of the National Weather Service, Melbourne office)

Plate 9. Hurricane Lili in the Florida Straits, 0749 EDT, October 18, 1996. (Courtesy of the National Aeronautics and Space Administration)

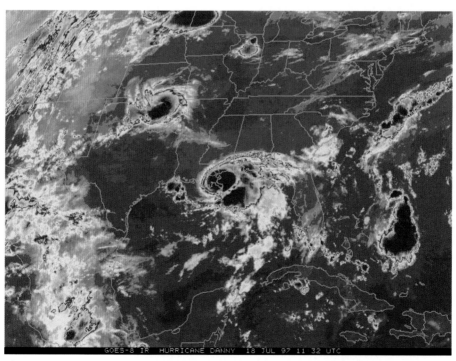

Plate 10. Hurricane Danny, 1132 GMT, July 18, 1997. (Courtesy of NOAA)

Plate 11. Hurricane Danny, 0018 GMT, July 19, 1997. (Courtesy of Johns Hopkins University, Applied Physics Laboratory)

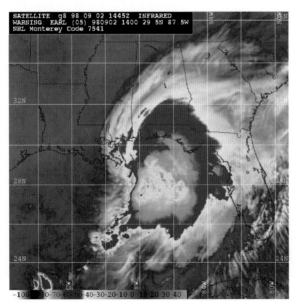

Plate 12. Hurricane Earl approaching Florida, IR image, 1445 GMT, September 2, 1998. (Courtesy of the Naval Research Laboratory, Monterey, California)

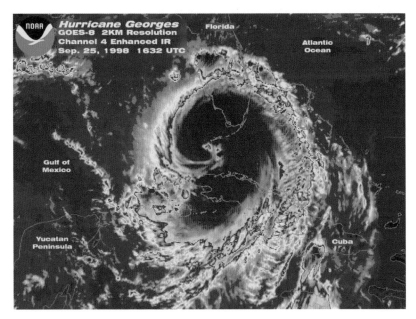

Plate 13. Hurricane Georges, IR image, 1632 GMT, September 25, 1998. (Courtesy of NOAA)

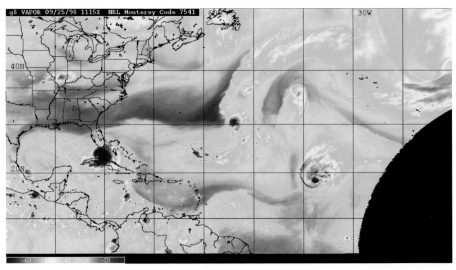

Plate 14. Hurricane Georges, water vapor image, 1115 GMT September 25, 1998; Hurricanes Ivan and Jeanne shown in center and at right, respectively. (Courtesy of Naval Research Laboratory, Monterey, California)

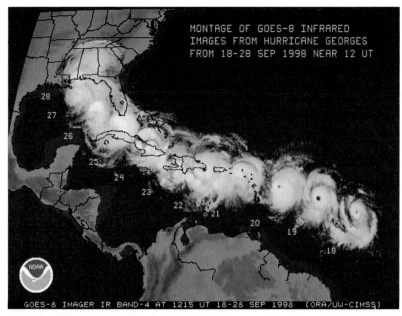

Plate 15. Hurricane Georges, montage of GOES 8 IR images, September 18–19, 1998. (Courtesy of NOAA)

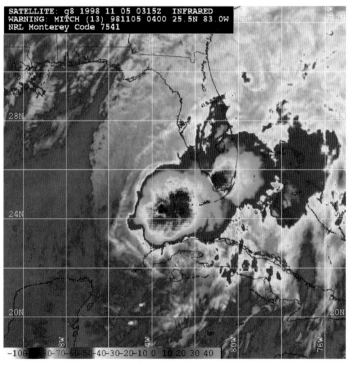

Plate 16. Hurricane Mitch approaches Florida, 0315 GMT, November 5, 1998. (Courtesy of the Naval Research Laboratory, Monterey, California)

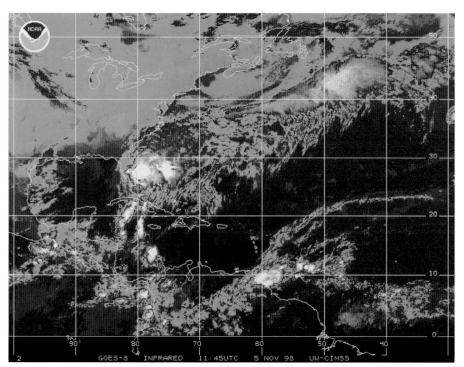

Plate 17. Hurricane Mitch, GOES 8 IR, after it had crossed Florida and was entering the Atlantic, 1145 GMT, November 5, 1998. (Courtesy of NOAA)

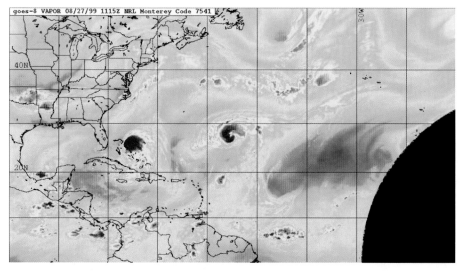

Plate 18. Hurricane Dennis in the Bahamas, August 27, 1999; Hurricane Cindy in mid-Atlantic (Courtesy of the Naval Research Laboratory, Monterey, California)

Plate 19. Hurricane Dennis, August 28, 1999. (Courtesy of the University of Wisconsin)

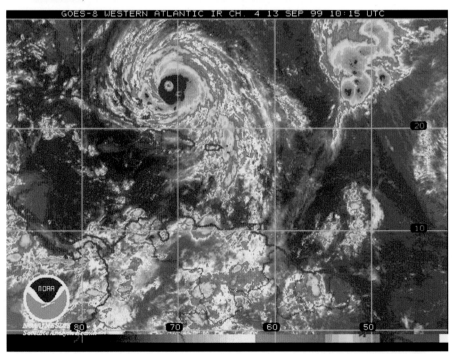

Plate 20. Hurricane Floyd, 1015 GMT, September 13, 1999. (Courtesy of NOAA)

Plate 21. Hurricane Floyd at its peak, 1200 GMT, September 13, 1999. (Courtesy of NOAA)

Plate 22. Tropical Storm Harvey shows a weak landfall near Naples, 1215 GMT, September 20, 1999. (Courtesy of the National Weather Service, Melbourne office)

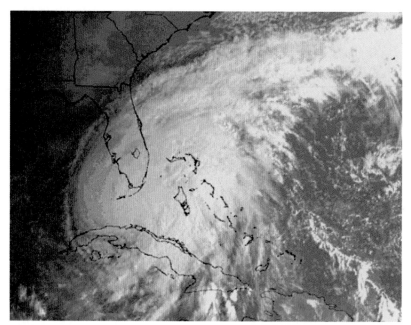

Plate 23. Hurricane Irene moving into the Atlantic just east of Melbourne, Florida, October 16, 1999. (Courtesy of the National Weather Service, Melbourne office)

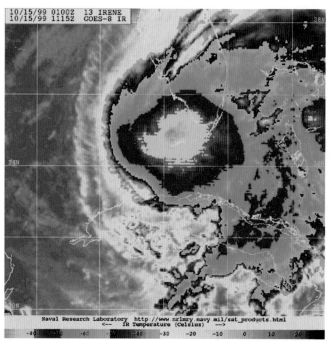

Plate 24. Hurricane Irene approaching southwest Florida, 1115 GMT, October 15, 1999. (Courtesy of the Naval Research Laboratory, Monterey, California)

Plate 25. Radar image of Hurricane Irene once it moved into the Atlantic just east of Melbourne, October 16, 1999. (Courtesy of the National Weather Service, Melbourne office)

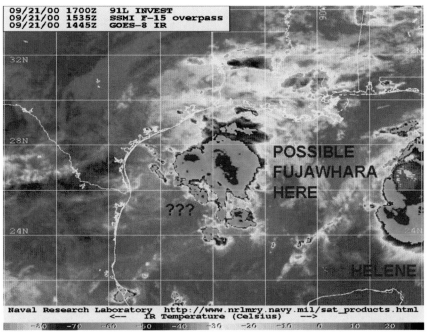

Plate 26. Tropical Storm Helene making landfall near Fort Walton Beach on the morning of September 22, 2000; the disturbance at left is a possible Fujawhara effect. (Courtesy of the Naval Research Laboratory, Monterey, California)

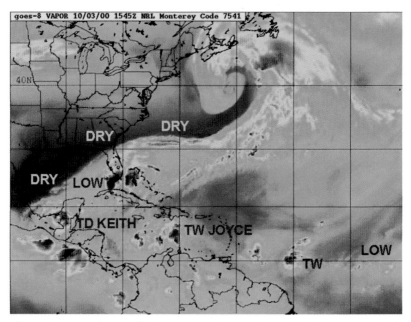

Plate 27. "Low" denotes the beginning of Tropical Storm Leslie's system developing, October 3, 2000; Keith and Joyce did not affect Florida. (Courtesy of the Naval Research Laboratory, Monterey, California)

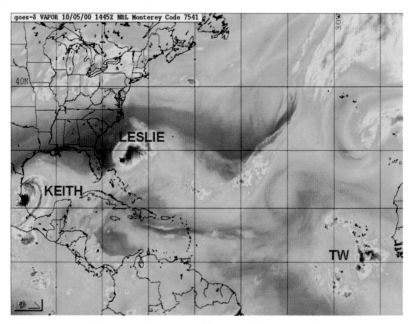

Plate 28. Tropical Storm Leslie, now a full tropical storm, just east of St. Augustine, October 5, 2000 (Courtesy of the Naval Research Laboratory, Monterey, California)

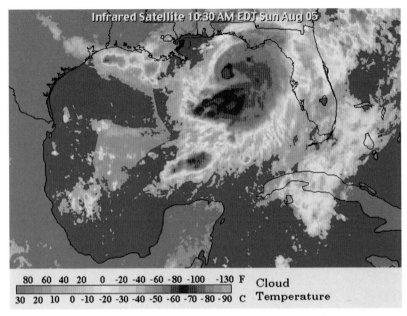

80 60 40 20 0 -20 -40 -60 -80 -100 -130 F Cloud
30 20 10 0 -10 -20 -30 -40 -50 -60 -70 -80 -90 C Temperature

Plate 29. Tropical Storm Barry approaching northwest Florida at 10:30 A.M. EDT, August 5, 2001. (Courtesy of the University of Michigan)

Plate 30. Tropical Storm Gabrielle approaching the southwest Florida coast at 7:15 A.M. DST, September 13, 2001. (Courtesy of the Naval Research Laboratory, Monterey, California)

Plate 31. Hurricane Michelle passing over Cuba. moving north-northeast on November 4, 2001. (Courtesy of the Naval Research Laboratory, Monterey, California)

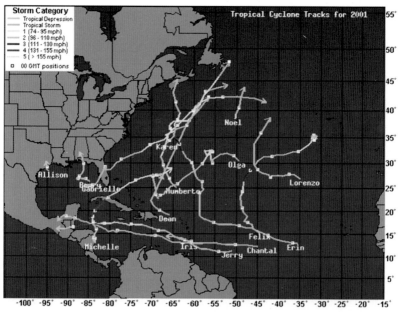

Plate 32. Final track, 2001 hurricane season. (Courtesy of the University of Michigan)

Internet References

FAQ: Hurricanes, Typhoons, and Tropical Cyclones
http://www.aoml.noaa.gov/hrd/tcfaq/tcfaqHED.html

John Williams's Weather FTP Site
ftp://duedall.fit.edu/williams/latestwx

National Hurricane Center
http://www.nhc.noaa.gov/

National Weather Service, Melbourne, Florida
http://www.srh.noaa.gov/mlb/

Tropical Meteorology
http://typhoon.atmos.colostate.edu/weather/

Weather Channel
http://www.weather.com

Wunderground.com Tropical Weather
http://www.wunderground.com/tropical/

Tables

Table 1. Saffir/Simpson Scale for classifying hurricanes

Category	Pressure		Winds (mph)	Surge (ft.)	Damage
	millibars	inches			
1	980	28.94	74–95	4–5	Minimal
2	965–979	28.50–28.91	96–110	6–8	Moderate
3	945–964	27.91–28.47	111–130	9–12	Extensive
4	920–944	27.17–27.88	131–155	13–18	Extreme
5	<920	<27.17	>155	>18	Catastrophic

Table 2. Hurricane classification prior to 1970 (for reference only)[a]

Hurricane intensity	Maximum winds (mph)	Minimum central pressure (in.)
Minor	74	29.40
Minimal	75–100	29.03–29.39
Major[b]	101–35	28.01–29.02
Extreme[c]	136	28.00

a. This classification was used to rate intensities of hurricanes through about 1970 and was replaced by the Saffir/Simpson Scale (table 1). Adapted from Dunn and Miller, 1964.

b. Major Hurricane: A hurricane with winds 111 mph or more is now referred to as a Category 3 or higher hurricane as classified by the Saffir/Simpson Scale.

c. Extreme Hurricane: An Extreme or Great Hurricane is one of great intensity (winds 125 mph or more) and great size (diameter of hurricane wind 100 miles or more) and characterized by other factors, such as minimum pressure, storm tides, destruction, and fatalities (R. W. Gray, 1933, as revised by Norton, 1949). The term *Great Hurricane* was used to classify storms through 1970 and is not used today. Norton (1949) classified 10 hurricanes as Great between 1880 and 1948:

August 1880: Palm Beach–Lake Okeechobee

June 1886: Apalachicola-Tallahassee

October 1890: Key West–Ft. Myers

July 1916: Pensacola-Mobile

September 1919: Key West

September 1926: Miami-Pensacola

September 1928: Palm Beach–Lake Okeechobee

September 1935: Great Labor Day Hurricane, Florida Keys

October 1944: Key West–Tampa–Jacksonville

September 1947: Ft. Lauderdale–Ft. Myers

Table 3. Number of hurricanes, tropical storms, and combined total storms by 10-year periods

Period	Hurricanes	Tropical storms	Combined
1871–1880	a	a	21
1881–1890	a	a	21
1891–1900	9	11	20
1901–1910	5	13	18
1911–1920	6	4	10
1921–1930	9	3	12
1931–1940	6	12	18
1941–1950	13	7	20
1951–1960	3	10	13
1961–1970	7	4	11
1971–1980	3	1	4
1981–1990	3	7	10
1991–2000	11	9	20
2001	0	2	2
Total	75	83	200

a. Includes 21 tropical cyclones of unknown intensity occurring between 1871–1880 and 1881–1890.

Table 4. Florida hurricanes, 1871–2001

Date	Name/ category	Area affected	Peak winds (mph)	Minimum pressure (inches)	Maximum surge (feet)	Damage, deaths, other data
1871 August	Not named	Cocoa Beach	Unknown	Unknown	Unknown	Not confirmed as a full hurricane. Direct hit, east-central Florida. (Frank 1978)
1873 October	Major	20 miles SSE of Venice	Unknown	Unknown	14	Punta Rassa, Florida destroyed. From west coast, across state to direct hit east-central Florida. (Dunn and Miller 1964)
1876 September	Not named	Eau Gallie (Melbourne)	Unknown	Unknown	Unknown	Indirect hit east-central Florida. (Frank 1978; Holmes 1876)
1880 August	Major	Cocoa Beach	Unknown	Unknown	Unknown	Severe damage at Palm Beach and Lake Okeechobee. Direct hit east-central Florida. (Frank 1978; Norton 1949)
1885 August	Not named	20 miles east of Cocoa Beach	Unknown	Unknown	Unknown	Indirect hit east-central Florida. (Rabac 1986)
1886 June	Major	Apalachicola	Unknown	Unknown	Unknown	High tides. (NOAA 1999; Norton 1949)
July	Not named	St. Marks North of Cedar Key	Unknown	Unknown	Unknown	Unknown. (NOAA 1999)
July	Not named		Unknown	Unknown	Unknown	Unknown. (NOAA 1999)

Note: This chronological list for Florida includes only hurricane-strength storms. Values for category, peak winds (gusts), minimum pressure, maximum surge, and damage and deaths refer to the most extreme conditions regardless of location of the storm and category.

Date	Name	Location				Notes
1887 July	Not named	Valparaiso	Unknown	Unknown	Unknown	Unknown. (NOAA 1999)
1888 August	Not named	Miami	Unknown	Unknown	14	Unknown. (NOAA 1999)
October	Not named	Cedar Key	Unknown	Unknown	Unknown	Nine died. (Dunn and Miller 1964; NOAA 1999)
1889 September	Not named	Pensacola	Unknown	Unknown	Unknown	Unknown. (NOAA 1999)
1891 August	Not named	Miami	Unknown	Unknown	Unknown	Unknown. (NOAA 1999)
1893 June	Not named	Cross City	Unknown	Unknown	Unknown	Unknown. (NOAA 1999)
1894 September	Major	Key West, Punta Gorda	104 Key West	Unknown	Unknown	Unknown. (Dunn and Miller 1964; NOAA 1999)
October	Not named	Apalachicola	Unknown	Unknown	Unknown	Unknown. (NOAA 1999)
1896 July	Major	Pensacola	100	Unknown	Unknown	Unknown. (Dunn and Miller 1964; NOAA 1999)
September	Major	Cedar Key	Unknown	Unknown	10 Cedar Key	100 deaths in Florida. (Dunn and Miller 1964; NOAA 1999)
October	Not named	Punta Gorda	Unknown	Unknown	Unknown	68 deaths with over $2 million in damages. From west coast across state to direct hit east-central Florida. (NOAA 1999)
1898 August	Not named	Apalachicola	Unknown	Unknown	10.8 Fernandina Beach	12 deaths and $100,000 in damages. (U.S. Weather Bureau 1898)
1899 August	Cat. 2	Carrabelle	Unknown	28.90	3–4	Six deaths with $500,000 in damages. Seven ships wrecked. (USWB 1899)

Date	Name/category	Area affected	Peak winds (mph)	Minimum pressure (inches)	Maximum surge (feet)	Damage, deaths, other data
1903						
September	Cat. 1	Jupiter, Apalachicola	78	29.46	8–10	14 deaths with $500,000 in damages. Ship wrecked near Jupiter. (USWB 1903)
1906						
September	Cat. 2	Pensacola	100	28.29	10	34 deaths in Pensacola, 134 total deaths, $3–4 million in damages. (USWB 1906)
October	Cat. 2	Key West, Miami	Unknown	28.55 Miami	Unknown	A total of 164 railroad workers dead in Miami with $160,000 in damages. (USWB 1906)
1909						
October	Cat. 3	Key West	Unknown	28.26 Marathon	Unknown	15 deaths with $1 million in damages. (USWB 1906)
1910						
October	Cat. 3	Key West, Ft. Myers	125 Sand Key	28.20 Ft. Myers	15 Key West	30 deaths with $365,000 in damages. This hurricane looped in the Gulf of Mexico. (Tannehill 1938; Dunn and Miller 1964)
1911						
August	Cat. 1	Pensacola	Unknown	Unknown	Unknown	Unknown. (USWB 1911)
1915						
September	Cat. 1	Apalachicola	Unknown	29.25	Unknown	21 deaths and $100,000 in damages. Wrecked sponge vessels. (USWB 1915)
1916						
October	Cat. 2	NW Florida	120	28.76	Unknown	Tower blown down at Pensacola and $100,000 in damages. (USWB 1916)
November	Cat. 1	Florida Keys	75	Unknown	Unknown	Unknown. (USWB 1917; Hebert et al. 1995)
1917						
September	Cat. 3	Pensacola	125	28.29	7.5	Unknown. (USWB 1917; Hebert et al. 1995)

1919						
September	Cat. 4	Key West	115	27.37 Key West	Unknown Dry Tortugas	More than 600 died (300 in Key West) and $2 million in damages. Key West anemometer destroyed. (USWB 1919; Hebert et al. 1995)
1921						
October	Cat. 3	Tarpon Springs	100 Tarpon Springs	28.11 Tarpon Springs	10.5 Tampa	Six deaths and $3 million in damages. Highest surge since 1848. From west coast across state to Ponce de Leon Inlet. Indirect hit on east-central Florida.
1924						
September	Cat. 1	Port St. Joe	Unknown	29.12	Unknown	Damages of $275 million. (USWB 1924)
October	Cat. 1	Marco Island	90	28.80	Unknown	Unknown. (USWB 1924)
1925						
November	Cat. 1	Sarasota, Tampa	Unknown	29.5	Unknown	50 deaths and $1.6 million in damages. Latest storm to strike U.S. Only one hurricane and one tropical storm in 1925. (USWB 1925)
1926						
July	Cat. 2	Jupiter, Indian River Lagoon	90	28.80	Unknown	$3 million in damages. Direct hit east-central Florida. (USWB 1926; *Melbourne Times* Anon. 1926)
September	Cat. 4	Miami, Pensacola	138 Miami	27.61 Miami	13.2 Miami	243 deaths with $1.4 billion (1990) in damages. (NHC-31 1995)
1928						
August	Cat. 2	Stuart, Indian River Lagoon	Unknown	28.84	Unknown	Two deaths and $250,000 in damages. Direct hit east-central Florida. (USWB 1928; *Melbourne Times* Anon. 1928)
September	Cat. 4 at Lake Okeechobee	Palm Beach, Lake Okeechobee	100+	27.43	10–15	1,836 dead and $26 million in damages. (USWB 1928; Hebert et al. 1995)

Date	Name/category	Area affected	Peak winds (mph)	Minimum pressure (inches)	Maximum surge (feet)	Damage, deaths, other data
1929						
September	Cat. 3	Marathon, Panama City	150	27.99	9	Three deaths and $821,000 in damages. (USWB 1929; Hebert et al. 1995)
1933						
July–August	Cat. 1	Florida east coast	95	28.96	Not known	(NOAA 1999)
September	Cat. 3	Jupiter	125	27.98	Unknown	Two deaths and $4 million in damages. (USWB 1933; Hebert et al. 1995)
1935						
September	Great Labor Day Hurricane Cat. 5	Long Key	200–250	26.35 Record in this hemisphere	20+	First category 5 on record to strike U.S. First and only category 5 to strike Florida; 408 deaths with $6 million in damages. (USWB 1935; Hebert et al. 1995; Norton 1949)
November	Yankee Hurricane Cat. 2	Miami	75 Miami	28.73 Miami	6	19 deaths and $5.5 million in damages. (USWB 1935; Hebert et al. 1995; Norton 1949)
1936						
July	Cat. 3	Ft. Walton Beach	125	28.46	6	Four deaths with $200,000 in damages. (USWB 1936; Hebert et al. 1995)
1939						
August	Cat.1	SE and NW Florida	80	Not known		(NOAA 1999)
1941						
October	Cat. 2	Miami, Carrabelle	123 Miami	28.48	8	Five deaths with $700,000 in damages. This hurricane looped in the Atlantic. (USWB 1941)

Year / Month	Category	Location	Wind	Pressure	Storm surge	Notes
1944						
October	Cat. 3	Sarasota	163	28.02 Dry Tortugas	12.3 Jacksonville	18 deaths with $582 million in damages. (USWB 1944; Norton 1949)
1945						
June–July	Cat. 3	NW Florida	115			(NOAA 1999)
September	Cat. 3	Homestead	196 Homestead	28.08	13.7	Four deaths with $540 million (1990) in damages. (USWB 1945)
1946						
October	Cat. 1	Bradenton	80	28.95	6	$7 million in damages. (USWB 1946)
1947						
September	Cat. 4	Pompano Beach	155 Hillsboro	27.76	21.6 Clewiston	Record wind speed recorded to date in Florida; 51 deaths with $704 million (1990) in damages. (USWB 1947; Norton 1949)
October	Cat. 1	Cape Sable	95	28.76	Unknown	One death with $20 million in damages. (USWB 1947)
1948						
September	Cat. 3	Key West, Everglades	122	28.45	19 Canal Point	Three deaths with $18 million in damages. (USWB 1948)
October	Cat. 3	Florida Keys, Homestead	100	28.44	6.2 Homestead	$5.5 million in damages. (USWB 1948)
1949						
August	Cat. 3	West Palm Beach, Stuart, Lake Okeechobee	153	28.17	24 Belle Glade	Two deaths with $52 million in damages. (USWB 1949)

Date	Name/category	Area affected	Peak winds (mph)	Minimum pressure (inches)	Maximum surge (feet)	Damage, deaths, other data
1950						
August	Baker Cat. 3	Florida Panhandle	125	28.90	Unkown	(NOAA 1999)
September	Easy Cat. 3	Cedar Key	125	28.29	6.5	Two deaths with $3.3 million in damage. Double loop in Gulf of Mexico just off Cedar Key, 38.7 inches rain in Yankeetown. (NOAA 1982)
October	King Cat. 3	Miami, Ft. Lauderdale	150	28.20	19.3 Clewiston	Three deaths with $28 million in damages. Indirect hit east-central Florida. (USWB 1950)
1953						
September	Florence Cat. 1	Ft. Walton Beach	87	Unknown	Unknown	Damages of $200,000. (USWB 1953)
1956						
September	Flossy Cat. 1	Ft. Walton Beach	98	28.93	6.1	15 deaths with $25 million in damages. Possibly formed from storm in Pacific. Three tornadoes in Florida. (USWB 1956; Dunn and Miller 1964)
1960						
September	Donna Cat. 4	Sombrero Key, Ft. Myers	180–200 Florida Keys	27.46	13 Flamingo 13.7 Tavenier	50 deaths with $1.823 billion (1990) in damages. Indirect hit east-central Florida. (USWB 1960; Hebert et al. 1995)
1964						
August	Cleo Cat. 2	Miami, Ft. Lauderdale, east coast U.S.	138	28.5	6	Three deaths with almost $600 million (1990) in damages. This was a "text-book" Cape Verde storm. The eye was 8–16 miles in diameter.

September	Dora Cat. 2	St. Augustine, North Florida	125	28.52	12	near Miami. Tornadoes reported from Davie to Daytona Beach. Indirect hit east-central Florida. (USWB 1964) Five deaths with over $1 billion (1990) in damages. Tides over 10 feet at Fernandina Beach, 10.7 inches of rain in Gainesville, 18.6 inches of rain at Live Oak; 23.7 inches at Mayo. The rain continued in some areas for four days. (USWB 1964)
October	Isbell Cat. 1	SW, SE, central Florida	90	28.47	4–5	Three deaths with heavy damage to vegetable crop. Small storm spawning many tornadoes in Florida, at least 11 along SE Florida coast. (USWB 1964)
1965 September	Betsy Cat. 3	South Florida Keys, Louisiana	165	27.82	9	75 deaths with over $6.4 billion (1990) in damages. Erratic course through Atlantic Ocean and Florida Straits. The eye was 40 miles in diameter at one time with 11.8 inches of rain at Plantation Key. (USWB 1965)
1966 June	Alma Cat. 2	Florida Panhandle, Southeast U.S.	125, Dry Tortugas	28.65	10	Eight deaths with nearly $10 million (1990) in damages. Earliest storm on record to hit U.S. to date. Rainfall of 7.7 inches in Miami and 6-foot tides at St. Marks. (USWB 1966)
October	Inez Cat. 4	South Florida, Florida Keys, Mexico	165, Big Pine Key	27.38	15.5	48 deaths with over $5 million (1990) in damages. Another storm with an erratic course. Category 4 in Caribbean. (USWB 1966)

Date	Name/ category	Area affected	Peak winds (mph)	Minimum pressure (inches)	Maximum surge (feet)	Damage, deaths, other data
1968 October	Gladys Cat. 2	NE Florida, Cedar Key	90	28.49	6.5	Damages of $7 million. Tides of 5 feet at Tampa and 6.6 inches of rain at Daytona. (ESSA 1968)
1972 June	Agnes Cat. 1	Port St. Joe	86	28.85	7	122 deaths with damages of $6 billion (1990). More than 1,000-mile diameter circulation. Spawned 15 tornadoes in Florida with 8.5 inches of rain at Key West and 12.7 inches of rain at Big Pine Key. (Hebert et al. 1995)
1975 September	Eloise Cat. 3	Midway between Ft. Walton Beach and Panama City	155	28.20	18	Nine deaths with $1.1 billion (1990) in damages. (Hebert et al. 1995)
1979 September	David Cat. 2, Cat. 4 in Caribbean	Jupiter, Indian River Lagoon, Vero Beach, Melbourne, Ft. Lauderdale, Pompano	172	27.28	3–5	Five deaths on U.S. mainland, seven in Puerto Rico, 1,200 in Dominican Republic, with $487,366,000 (1990) in damages. Direct hit east-central Florida as Cat. 2 hurricane. (Hebert et al. 1995)
1985 August– September	Elena Cat. 3	No landfall, closest	125 (aircraft)	28.17	8	Deaths unknown with $1.392 billion (1990) in damages. One million people were evacuated.

		point Cedar Key and Cape San Blas				from affected areas. Rainfall in Apalachicola was 11.3 inches. (Hebert et al. 1995)
October	Juan Cat. 1	Florida, Louisiana, Alabama	85	28.67	Unknown	Damages were $1.671 dollars (1990). Not hurricane force in Florida. (Hebert et al. 1995)
November	Kate Cat. 2	Mexico Beach, Florida, Panama City	135	28.14	8	Five deaths with $300 million (1990) in damages. First SE Florida warnings since Inez (1966) on November 18–19. (*Monthly Weather Review* 1985; in NHC)
1987						
October	Floyd Cat. 1	Key West, Key Largo, Marathon	80	29.32	Unknown	Deaths and damages unknown. (NOAA 1999)
1992						
August	Andrew Cat. 4	Bahamas, south Florida, Louisiana	175	27.23	16.89 Miami	48 deaths with $15–30 billion (1993) in damages. Most destructive natural disaster in U.S. history. Third lowest barometric pressure at landfall in U.S. (NOAA 1993)
1994						
November	Gordon Cat. 1	South and central Florida, North Carolina	85	28.94	3–5	Most of the 1,145 deaths occurred in Haiti with $400 million (1994) in damages. Gust at Guantanamo, Cuba, to 120 mph. (USWB 1995; Hebert et al. 1995). Not hurricane force in Florida.
1995						
June	Allison Cat. 1	Apalachi- cola,	75	29.15	Unknown	One death with $1.7 million damages. Strong tropical storm/possibly weak hurricane at

Date	Name/category	Area affected	Peak winds (mph)	Minimum pressure (inches)	Maximum surge (feet)	Damage, deaths, other data
		Panama City, St. Marks				landfall. Earliest storm on record to hit Florida Panhandle. (USWB 1995; Hebert et al. 1995)
1995						
July–August	Erin Cat. 1	Central and west coast Florida, Pensacola, Florida Panhandle	100	28.72	3–5	Nine deaths with $700 million in damages. The eye was 40 miles in diameter after landfall. A 234-foot gambling cruise ship east of Cape Canaveral sank, resulting in three deaths. (USWB 1995; Hebert et al. 1995)
September–October	Opal Cat. 4	Yucatan, Florida Panhandle, Alabama, Georgia	150	27.01	12	59 deaths and $3 billion in damages. Near Category 5 in the Gulf of Mexico and a Category 3 at landfall. Category 5 pressure. (USWB 1995; Hebert et al. 1995)
1996						
August	Fran Cat. 3	Florida east coast	120	28.35	4–6	Hurricane watch along Florida's east coast; 24 deaths and $3.2 billion in damages. Not hurricane force in Florida. (Avila and Pasch 1997)
October	Lili Cat. 3	Florida Keys	115	28.35	4–6	Hurricane watch in Florida Keys. Not hurricane force in Florida.
1997						
July	Danny Cat. 1	NW Florida, Panhandle	80	29.05	4–5	Four deaths with $100 million in damages. (Rappaport 1998)

1998						
August–September	Earl Cat. 2	Florida, Georgia	100	29.08	4–5	Three deaths with $79 million in damages. (Pasch 1999)
September	Georges Cat. 4	Caribbean islands, Cuba, Florida Keys, Alabama, Mississippi	155+	27.61	+6 in Florida Keys	602 deaths with a total $5.9 billion in damages; $3.5 billion in damages in Puerto Rico alone. (Pasch 1999)
October–November	Mitch Cat. 5	Central America, Mexico, Yucatan, Florida	180+	26.71	Unknown in Central America	More than 10,000 total deaths. $40 million in damages in Florida as a tropical storm. Tornadoes in Florida Keys. Mitch is only the sixth Category 5 storm in the Atlantic basin in the twentieth century. Not hurricane force in Florida. (Pasch 1999)
1999						
August–September	Dennis Cat. 2	Bahamas, Florida, North Carolina	105	28.39	6	Four deaths in Florida from high surf. $157 million in damages. Not hurricane force in Florida. (Lawrence et al. 2000)
September	Floyd Cat. 4	Bahamas, Florida, North Carolina, Northeast U.S.	155	27.16	Up to 10	57 deaths (56 in the U.S., 1 in Bahamas) with $3–6 billion in damages. Heavy surf in Florida east coast. 2 million people in Florida evacuated. (Lawrence et al. 2000)
October	Irene Cat. 2	Cuba, Florida, South Carolina, North Carolina	110	28.27	6–8	Eight people electrocuted/drowned in Florida. $800 million in damages.(Lawrence et al. 2000)

Date	Name/ category	Area affected	Peak winds (mph)	Minimum pressure (inches)	Maximum surge (feet)	Damage, deaths, other data
2000						
September	Gordon Cat. 1	Yucatan, Florida, Georgia, South Carolina	80	28.97	4	$11 million in damages. Probably tropical storm in Florida at landfall. Several tornadoes in central and south Florida. Not hurricane force in Florida. (Franklin and Avila 2001)
2001						
September	Gabrielle Cat. 1	Florida west coast, central state	80	29.02	Unknown	Landfall (as TS) near Tampa—to across state into Atlantic—2 deaths. (NHC website: www.nhc.noaa.gov 2001)

Figures

Fig. 1.A. A home in Coconut Grove after the Great Miami Hurricane, 1926. (Courtesy of National Hurricane Center)

Fig. 1.B. Meyer-Kiser Building, N.E. 1st Street, Miami, September 1926 hurricane. The building had to be torn down. (Courtesy of National Hurricane Center)

Fig. 1.C. Sunken boat, Miami, September 1926 hurricane. The boat was once owned by Kaiser Wilhelm of Germany. (Courtesy of National Hurricane Center)

Fig. 1.D. Damaged building, 1926 Miami hurricane. (Courtesy of Richard Clark)

Fig. 1.E. Used car lot, 1926 Miami hurricane. (Courtesy of Richard Clark)

Fig. 1.F. Pancoast Hotel, Miami Beach, 1926 Miami hurricane. (Courtesy of Richard Clark)

Fig. 1.G. A damaged home, 1926 Miami hurricane. (Courtesy of Richard Clark)

Fig. 1.H. A damaged home; 1926 Miami hurricane. (Courtesy of Richard Clark)

Fig. 1.I. The vessel *Rose Mahoney* at Ninth and Biscayne, 1926 Miami hurricane. (Courtesy of Richard Clark)

Fig. 2.A. Damage in Palm Beach, 1928 hurricane. (Courtesy of National Hurricane Center)

Fig. 2.B. Destruction in West Palm Beach, 1928 hurricane. (Courtesy of National Hurricane Center)

Fig. 3.A. Train blown off track in Islamorada, Florida Keys, Great Labor Day Hurricane, 1935.

Fig. 3.B. Flagler railroad track in Islamorada, Florida Keys, Great Labor Day Hurricane, 1935.

Fig. 3.C. Monument to hurricane of 1935, Islamorada, Florida Keys. (Courtesy of Iver Duedall)

Fig. 3.D. Inscription plaque commemorating those who died in the 1935 hurricane. (Courtesy of Iver Duedall)

Fig. 4.A. Hurricane Donna in 1960 did not strike Miami, but this photograph shows typical wave action along the Dade County shoreline. (Courtesy of National Hurricane Center)

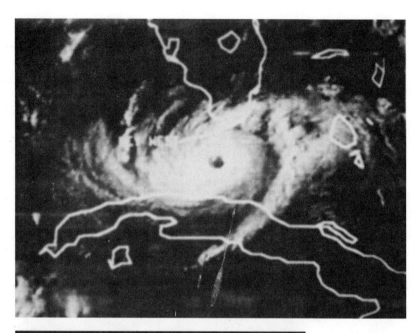

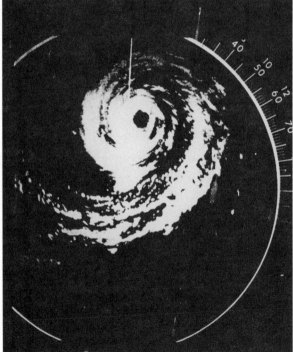

Fig. 4.B. Satellite picture of Hurricane Donna, 1960. (Courtesy of National Hurricane Center)

Fig. 4.C. Radar of Hurricane Donna, 1960. (Courtesy of National Hurricane Center)

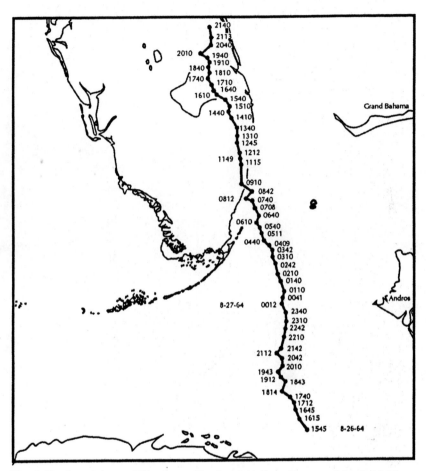

Fig. 5. Track and times of Hurricane Cleo in 1964 (from Dunn and Staff, 1967).

Fig. 6.A. View of 27th Avenue, Miami, Hurricane Betsy in 1965. (Courtesy of *Miami Herald*)

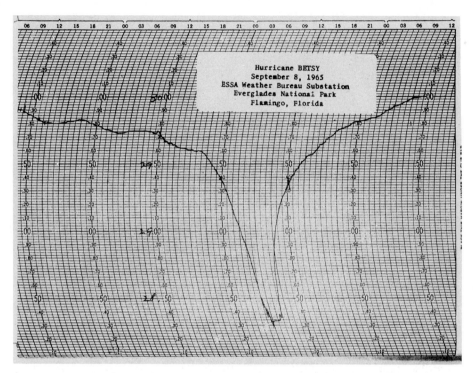

Fig. 6.B. Record of barometric pressure, Hurricane Betsy, 1965. (Courtesy of National Hurricane Center)

Fig. 7.A. Hurricane David in 1979 in the Caribbean. (Courtesy of Hank Brandli)

Fig. 7.B. Hurricane David in 1979 in Florida. (Courtesy of Hank Brandli)

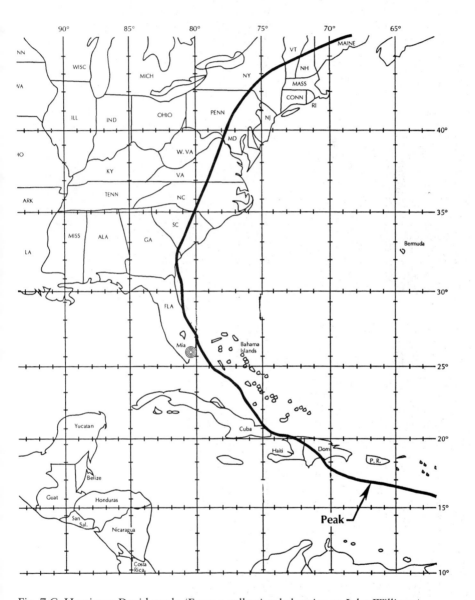

Fig. 7.C. Hurricane David track. (From a collection belonging to John Williams)

Fig. 8. Damage by Hurricane Elena, 1985 (from Clark, 1986a).

Fig. 9.A. Hurricane Juan damage (1985) (from Clark, 1986a).

Fig. 9.B. Hurricane Juan damage (1985) (from Clark, 1986a).

Fig. 9.C. Hurricane Juan damage (1985) (from Clark, 1986a).

Fig. 10.A. Hurricane Kate damage (1985) (from Clark, 1986b).

Fig. 10.B. Hurricane Kate damage (1985) (from Clark, 1986b).

Fig. 11.A. People standing in line for food and water after Hurricane Andrew, 1992. (Courtesy of Larry Floyd)

Fig. 11.B. One of the 39 debris-burning sites. (Courtesy of U.S. Army Corps of Engineers, 1993)

Fig. 11.C. The Last Chance Saloon on U.S. Highway 1 south of Homestead, Florida, has survived several hurricanes—Donna, Cleo, Betsy, and Andrew. Trees blown down to the left are the result of Andrew. (Courtesy of Iver W. Duedall)

Fig. 11.D. Roofs took a beating during Hurricane Andrew. (Courtesy of U.S. Army Corps of Engineers, 1993)

Fig. 11.E. Mobile home damage, Hurricane Andrew. (Courtesy of Larry Floyd)

Fig. 11.F. Residential roof damage, Hurricane Andrew. (Courtesy of Larry Floyd)

Fig. 11.G. Homestead Air Force Base, Hurricane Andrew. (Courtesy of Larry Floyd)

Fig. 11.H. Homestead Air Force Base, Hurricane Andrew. (Courtesy of Larry Floyd)

Fig. 11.I. Board "growing" in a palm tree, Hurricane Andrew, 1992.

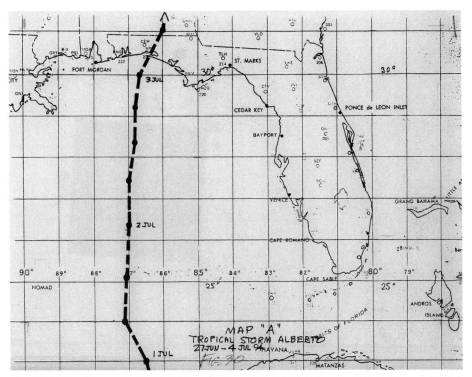

Fig. 12.A. Tracking map, Tropical Storm Alberto, Florida Panhandle, 1994. (Courtesy John Williams)

Fig. 12.B. Flooding from Alberto. (Courtesy National Hurricane Center)

Fig. 12.C. Satellite picture, Tropical Storm Alberto. (Courtesy of Hank Brandli)

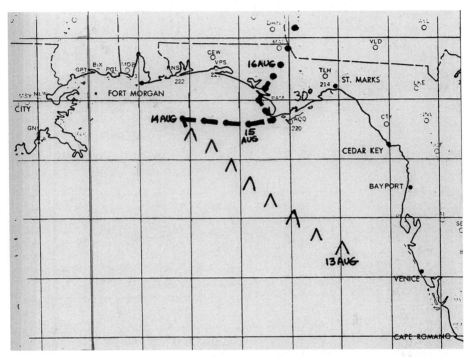

Fig. 13. Tracking map, Tropical Storm Beryl, Florida Panhandle, 1994. (Courtesy of John Williams)

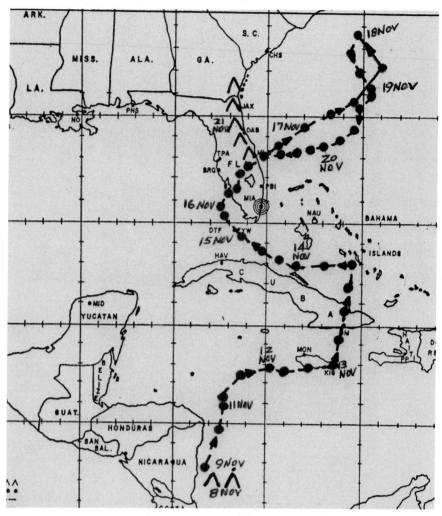

Fig. 14.A. Tracking map, Hurricane Gordon, Florida, 1994. (Courtesy of John Williams)

Fig. 14.B. Satellite photograph, Hurricane Gordon, 1994. (Courtesy of Hank Brandli)

Fig. 14.C. Satellite photograph, Hurricane Gordon, 1994. (Courtesy of Hank Brandli)

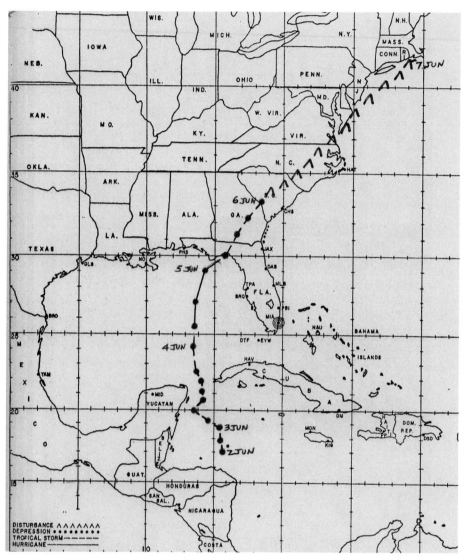

Fig. 15.A. Tracking map, Hurricane Allison, Florida Panhandle, 1995. (Courtesy of John Williams)

Fig. 15.B. Sunken shrimp boat at Eastpoint, Florida, Hurricane Allison, 1995. (Courtesy of Vern Miller, *Panama City News Herald*)

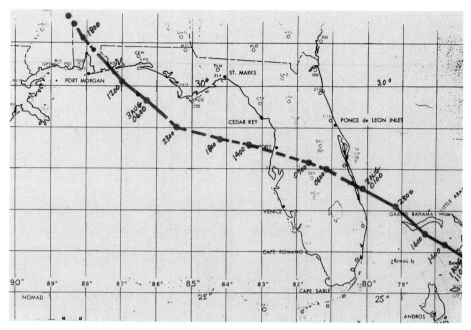

Fig. 16.A. Tracking map, Hurricane Erin, Florida, 1995. (Courtesy of John Williams)

Fig. 16.B. Satellite photograph, Hurricane Erin just before Florida landfall. (Courtesy of Hank Brandli)

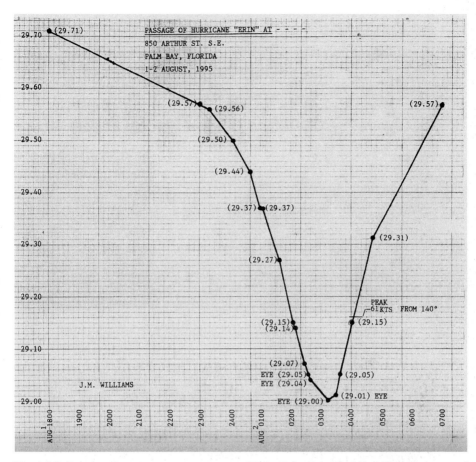

Fig. 16.C. Barometric pressure trace, passage of Erin, Palm Bay, Florida, 1995. (Courtesy of John Williams)

Fig. 16.D. Satellite photograph, Hurricane Erin, second landfall. (Courtesy of Hank Brandli)

Fig. 16.E. Hurricane Erin damage, 1995. (Courtesy of Laura Harris, *Panama City News Herald*)

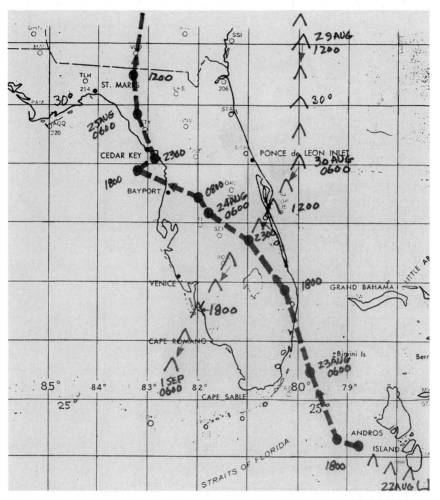

Fig. 17. Tracking map, Tropical Storm Jerry, Florida, 1995. (Courtesy of John Williams)

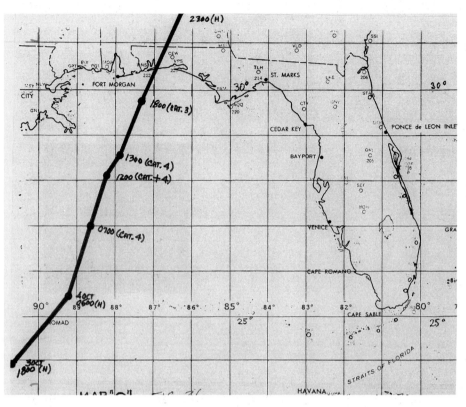

Fig. 18.A. Tracking map, Hurricane Opal, 1995. (Courtesy of John Williams)

Fig. 18.B. Panama City Beach, Florida, after Hurricane Opal. (Courtesy of Vern Miller, *Panama City News Herald*)

Fig. 18.C. Panama City Beach, Florida, after Hurricane Opal. (Courtesy of Vern Miller, *Panama City News Herald*)

Fig. 18.D. Panama City Beach after Hurricane Opal. (Courtesy of Tom Needham, *Panama City News Herald*)

Fig. 18.E. Mexico Beach, Florida, after Hurricane Opal. (Courtesy of Tracy Wilcox, *Panama City News Herald*)

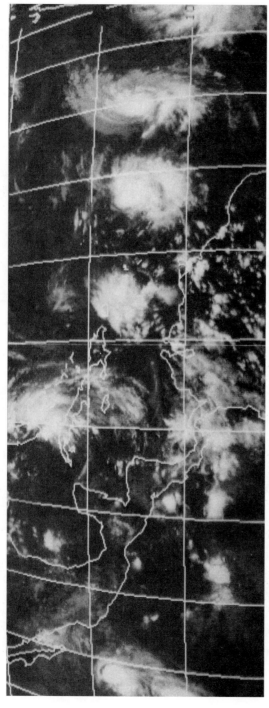

Fig. 19. Satellite photograph showing five 1995 storms at once. *Left to right*: Jerry (23 August), Iris (27 August), Karen (29 August), Humberto (25 August), and Luis (29 August). (Courtesy of National Hurricane Center)

Fig. 20.A. Damage on Key West by Hurricane Georges at Category 1.

Fig. 20.B. Damage on Big Pine Key by Hurricane Georges at Category 3.

Tracking Plates

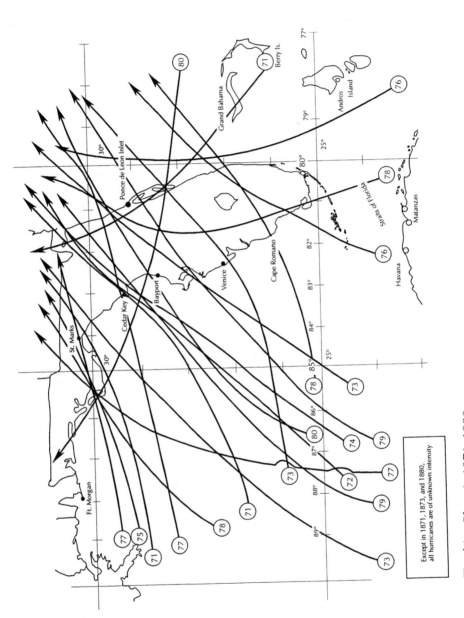

Except in 1871, 1873, and 1880, all hurricanes are of unknown intensity

Tracking Plate 1. 1871–1880

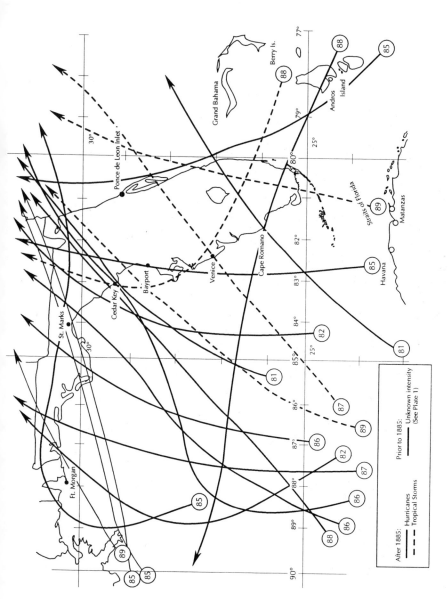

Tracking Plate 2. 1881–1890

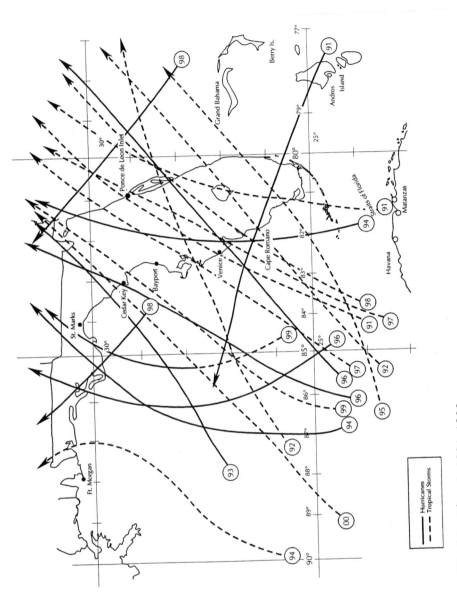

Tracking Plate 3. 1891–1900

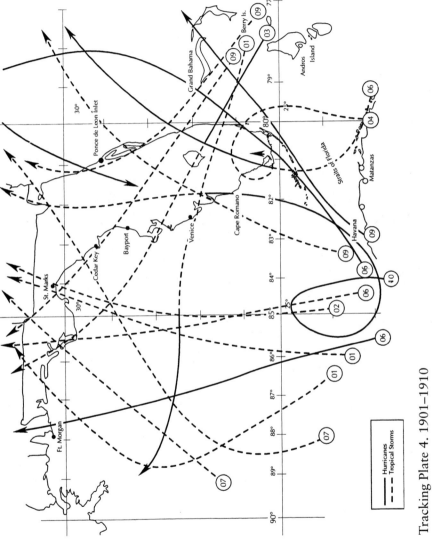

Tracking Plate 4. 1901–1910

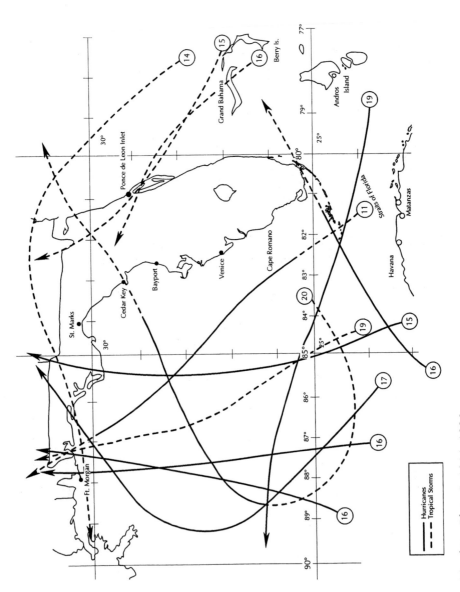

Tracking Plate 5. 1911–1920

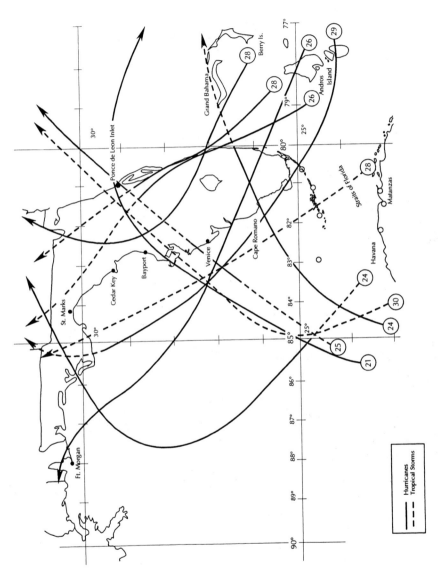

Tracking Plate 6. 1921–1930

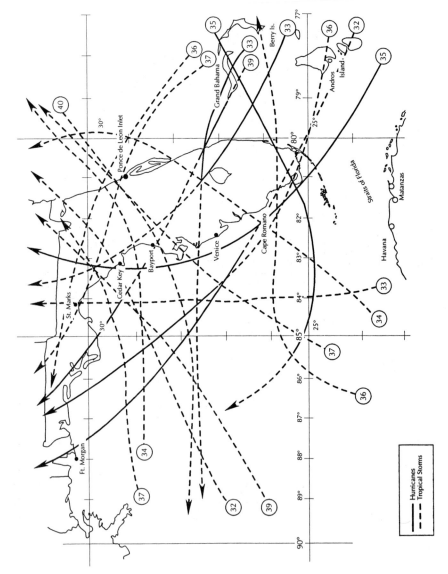

Tracking Plate 7. 1931–1940

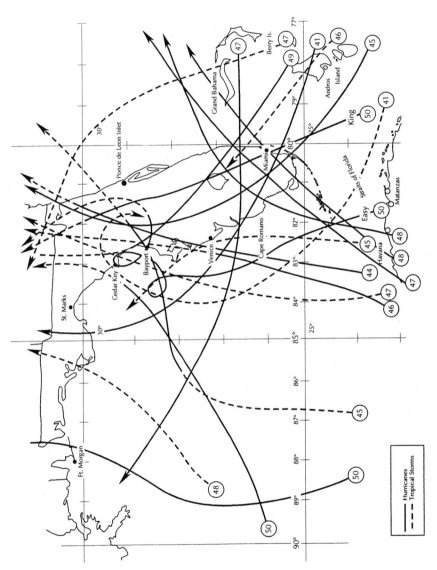

Tracking Plate 8. 1941–1950

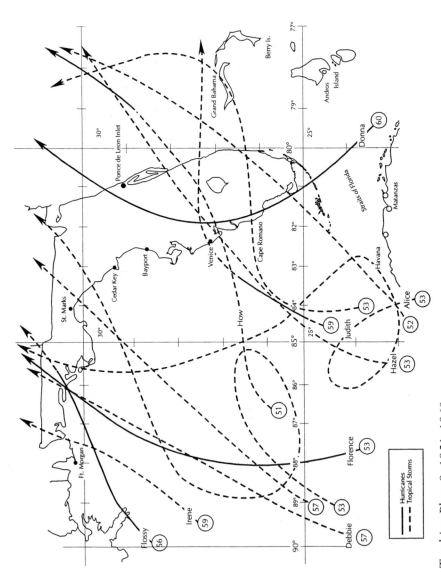

Tracking Plate 9. 1951–1960

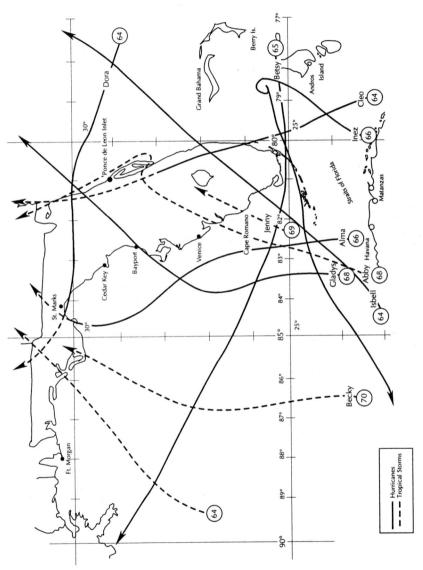

Tracking Plate 10. 1961–1970

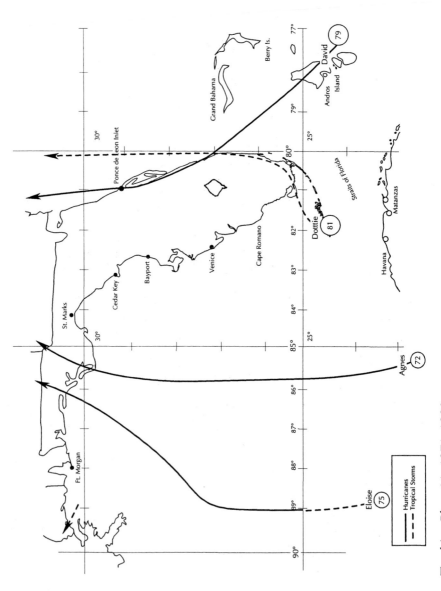

Tracking Plate 11. 1971–1980

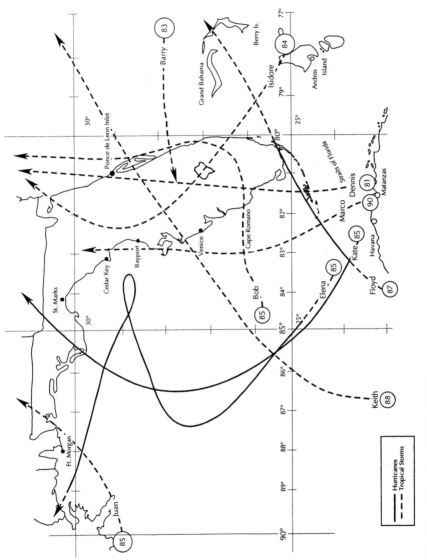

Tracking Plate 12. 1981–1990

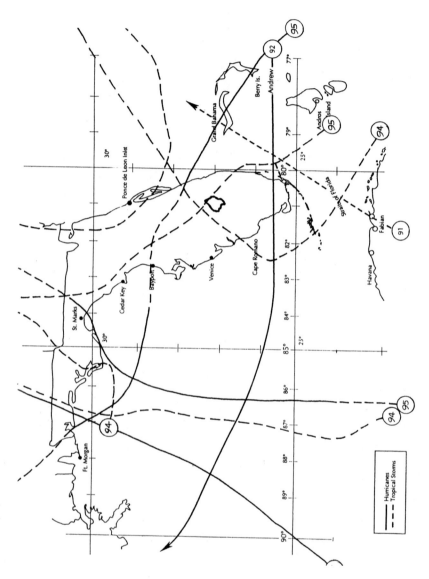

Tracking Plate 13. 1991–2000

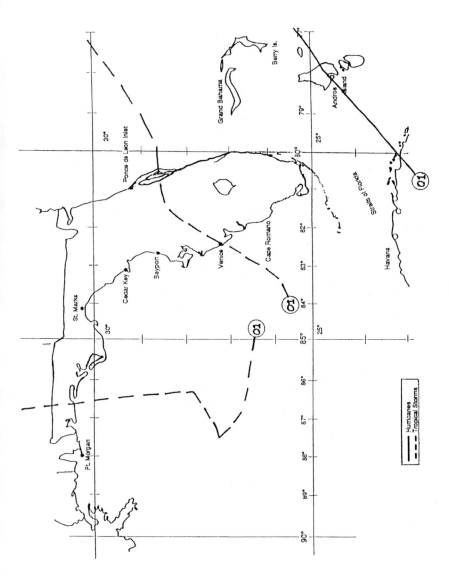

Tracking Plate 14. 2001

Index of Named Florida Hurricanes

Year	Month	Name	Highest Category	Page
1950	August	Baker	3	94
	September	Easy	3	22, 94, 151
	October	King	3	23–25, 27, 94, 152
1953	September	Florence	1	25, 49, 94, 152
1956	September	Flossy	1	25, 94, 152
1960	September	Donna	4	3, 7, 18, 25–26, 94, 111–12, 152
1964	August	Cleo	2	7, 27–28, 30–31, 94, 113, 153
	September	Dora	2	27–28, 30, 95, 153
	October	Isbell	1	12, 27, 30, 39, 95
1965	September	Betsy	3	12, 27, 30–31, 95, 114–15, 143
1966	June	Alma	2	27, 33–34, 95, 153
	October	Inez	4	12, 27, 32, 95, 153
1968	October	Gladys	2	27, 33–34, 96, 153
1972	June	Agnes	1	3, 35, 96, 154
1975	September	Eloise	3	27, 35, 52, 96, 154
1979	September	David	4	1, 27, 35–37, 54, 96, 116–17, 154
	August	Frederic*	3	37
1981	August	Dennis*	1	8, 37–38, 65, 99, 155, pl. 18, 19
1983	August	Barry*	1	8, 38, 53, 69, 155, pl. 29
1984	September	Diana*	3	38
1985	July	Bob*	1	36, 38, 41, 155
	August	Elena*	3	7, 27, 39, 96, 118, 155
	October	Juan	1	27, 39, 97
	November	Kate	2	27, 39, 97, 121, 155
1987	October	Floyd	1	8–9, 12, 38, 65–66, 97, 155, pl. 20, 21
1988	August	Chris*	1	39, 88
	November	Keith*	1	39, 88, pl. 27
1991	August	Bob*	2	36, 38, 41, 155
1992	August	Andrew	4	ix, 1, 2, 4, 17, 21, 25–27, 41–42, 46–48 , 97, 122–25, 156, pl. 1

(continued)

Year	Month	Name	Highest Category	Page
1994	November	Gordon*	1	xi, 41, 50–51, 67, 100, 130–31, pl. 2
1995	August	Allison*	1	33, 52–53, 57, 60, 67–69, 97, 132–33, pl. 3
	August	Erin	1	7–8, 52–57, 98, 134–36, pl. 4
	October	Opal	4	ix, 52, 57–58, 60, 98, 138–39, pl. 6–8
1996	September	Fran	3	59, 98
	October	Lili*	3	60, 70, 98, pl. 9
1997	July	Danny	1	8, 61, 98, pl. 10, 11
1998	Aug.–Sept.	Earl	2	8, 62, 98, pl. 12
	September	Georges	4	12, 63–64, 99, 142, pl. 13–15
	October	Mitch*	5	62, 64, 99, pl. 16.–17
1999	Aug.–Sept.	Dennis*	2	8, 37–38, 65, 99, 155, pl. 18, 19
	September	Floyd*	4	8, 12, 38, 65–66, 97, 99, 155, pl. 20, 21
	October	Irene	2	66, 99, 152, pl. 23–25
2000	September	Gordon	1	67, 100, 130–31, pl. 1
2001	September	Gabrielle*	1	8, 57, 69, 100, pl. 30

*Not hurricane status in Florida.

Subject Index

Note: A name in italic indicates a listing in the reference section.

Abby, 34, 153
Africa, 1, 68
Agnes, 3, 35, 96, 154
Alabama, 12, 48, 49, 57, 61, 97–98
Albany, Georgia, 49
Alberto, 41, 48–49, 127–128
Alice, 25, 152
Allen, 18
Alligator Point, 33
Allison, v, vii, viii, 33, 52–53, 57, 60,
    68–70, 97, 132–33, pl. 3
Alma, 27, 33–34, 95, 153
American Red Cross, 71
Andrew, viii, ix, 1, 2, 4, 15, 17, 21 25–27,
    41–42, 46–48, 52, 97, 122–25, 156,
    pl. 1
Antigua, 63
Antonini, G. A., et al., 79
Apalachicola, 12, 25, 33–35, 48–49, 53,
    56, 61, 86, 88–90, 97
Apalachicola Bay, 48, 49
Apalachicola River, 48
Atlantic basin, 1, 19, 52, 60, 65
Atlantic Ocean, 6–7, 58
Australia, 1
Avila, L. A. See J. Franklin and L. Avila;
    M. Lawrence et al.
Avila, L. A., and R. J. Pasch, 79

Baguios, 1
Bahamas, 18, 31, 42, 48, 50, 53, 56, 60,
    97, 99, pl. 18
Bahia Mar Marina, 27

Baker, 94
Barbados, 37
Barry, viii, 38, 53, 69, 155, pl. 29
Barefoot Bay, 16, 50
Baton Rouge, 43
Bay of Campeche, 57–58
Bay of Pigs, 70
Bayport, 33, 34
Becky, 34, 153
Belize, 64
Belle Glade, 22, 93
Beryl, vii, 41, 49, 129
Bertha, 59
Bermuda, 70
Betsy, 27, 30–31, 95, 114–15
Beven, J., 70, 80. See also *M. Lawrence et al.*
Big Bend, 59
Bigelow, F. H., 10, 79
Big Pine Key, 64, 66, 95, 142
Biscayne Bay, 16, 46–47
Boca Chica Naval Air Station, 63
Bob, 36, 38, 41, 155
Box, P. W. See G. A. Antonini et al.
Bradenton, 93, 69
Brady, E. See G. A. Antonini et al.
Brandli, H., 116
Brenda, 25, 34
Brevard County, 17, 36, 69
Broward County, 50
Burpee, Robert, xi

Camille, 3, 18, 20, 34, 47
Canaveral Light House, 8

161

Cancun, 53
Cape Canaveral, 9, 21, 22, 31, 34, 36, 38, 40, 51, 56, 60, 69
Cape Hatteras, 38, 51, 69, 48
Cape Kennedy, 31, 34. *See also* Cape Canaveral
Cape Race, Newfoundland, 48
Cape Romano, 11, 57
Cape Sable, 93
Cape San Blas, 39, 49
Cape Verde, 1, 28, 31–32, 37, 42, 63–64, 94
Caribbean, 1, 6, 7, 14, 22, 24, 32–33, 57, 60, 63–64, 68, 70 95–96, 99
Carrabelle, 11, 89, 92
Carrodus, R. L. See A. L. Sugg et al.
Carysfort Reef Light, 21
Cedar Key, 22, 34, 37, 39, 49, 57–58, 67, 88–89, 94, 96–97
Central America, 99
Central Florida, 8
Chantal, 53
Charlotte County, 69
China Sea, 1
Chipola River, 48
Chris, 39, 49
Clark, Richard, 16, 79, 118–19, 120–21
Clarke, M. See G. A. Antonini et al.
Climatological Data Bulletins, 11
Clearwater, 34
Cleo, vii, 27–31, 94, 113, 153
Clewiston, 21, 23, 93–94
Club Royale, 56
Cocoa Beach, 8, 88
Coconut Grove, 101
Colorado State University, 59, 68
Conch Capital 12
Conch Key, 26
Coral Gables, 42, 47
Cozumel, 53, 57
Cross City, 57, 89
Crystal River, 33
Cuba, 11, 21–22, 23, 28, 30, 32–34, 38, 48, 50, 53, 57, 60, 63, 66, 70, 99
Cyclone, 1

Dade County, 46, 50, 111
Dania, 24
Danny, viii, 61, 98, pl. 10, 11
David, vii, 27, 35–37, 54, 96, 116–17, 154
Daytona, 38, 96
Daytona Beach, 26, 68, 95
Dean, 53
Debbie, 25, 49, 152
Dennis, viii, 37–38, 65, 99, 155, pl. 18, 19
Destin, 48, 61–62, 58
Diana, 38
Dinner Key Marina, 47
Disney World, 54
Dolly, 34
Dominica, 37
Dominican Republic, 37, 63, 96
Donna, vii, 3, 18, 25–26, 94, 111–12, 152
Doppler radar, ix, pl. 1, 2, 4
Dora, 27–28, 30, 95, 153
Dottie, 36, 154
Dry Tortugas, 14, 20, 33, 38, 68, 01, 93
Duedall, I., 54, 123
Dunn, G. E., and B. I. Miller, xi, 8, 11, 25–26, 79, 86, 88, 89
Dunn and Staff, 79
Duryee, Maj. W.B.C., 10

Earl, viii, 62, 98, pl. 12
Eastpoint, 133
Eastern Pacific Ocean, 1
Easy, 12, 94, 151
Eau Gallie, 9, 88
Eggmond, 15
Edouard, 59
Eglin Air Force Base, 35–36, 69
El Niño, 60, 62
El Salvador, 64
Elena, vii, 27, 39, 96, 118, 155
Eloise, 27, 35, 52, 96, 154
Eleuthera Island, 47
Emily, 47–48
Erin, vii–viii, 52–57, 98, 134–36, pl. 4
Ernesto, 49
Evacuation, 73
Everglades, 18, 93
Everglades City, 21, 26

Everglades National Park, 26
Extreme Hurricane, 5, 18, 86
Eye, of hurricane, 2, 9

Fabian, 41, 156
Fellsmere, 27
Felix, 52, 57
Fernandina Beach, 6, 9, 10, 30, 39, 89, 95
Flagler Railroad, 20
Flamingo, 26, 66, 94
Flint River, 48
Florence, 25, 49, 94, 152
Florida Institute of Technology, 43
Florida International University, xi
Florida Keys, 3, 13, 20, 25, 33, 42, 47,
    60, 70, 86, 90, 93–94, 98–99, 108
Florida Panhandle, 9, 35, 39, 49, 53, 59
    61–62, 68, 94–95, 98, 129
Florida Power and Light, 46
Florida Straits, 22, 28, 30, 32, 34, 48, 50,
    57, 60, 63, 66, 68, 95
Florida Today, 8
Flossy, 25, 94, 152
Floyd, viii–ix, 12, 38, 65–66, 97, 99, 155,
    pl. 20, 21
Floyd, L., 112, 125
Fowey Rocks (Biscayne Bay), 43, 57
Fran, 59, 98
Frank, Neil, xi, 8, 79, 88
Franklin, J. See J. Lawrence et al.
Franklin, J., and L. Avila, 67, 79, 100
Franklin County, 12
Frederic, 37
Ft. Lauderdale, 22–23, 27–28, 30–32, 37,
    47, 86, 94, 96
Ft. Myers, 11, 20, 26, 34, 38, 40, 42, 50,
    86, 90
Ft. Pierce, 19
Ft. Walton Beach, 25, 35–36, 67, 92, 94,
    96
Fujawhara Effect, 68, 76
Fujita, Theodore, ix
Fujita Tornado Scale, ix, 4–5

Gabrielle, viii, 57, 69, 100, pl. 30
Gainesville, 95

Galt, Florida, 13
Galveston, Texas, 15, 68
Garriott, E. B., 6, 8, 79
Georgia, 21, 27, 38, 48, 49, 51, 68, 98,
    100
Georges, 12, 63–64, 99, 142, pl. 13–15
Gilbert, 2, 19
Gladys, 27, 33–34, 96, 153
GOES, 36, 61, 76
Goldenberg, S. B., et al., 3, 80
Good Year Blimp Base, 43
Gordon, 41, 50–51, 67, 100, 130–31,
    pl. 2
Grand Bahamas Island, 22
Grassy Key, 30
Gray, R. W., xi, 86
Gray, W. M., 2, 59, 80. See also S. B.
    Goldenberg et al.
Great Hurricane, xii, 5, 8, 11, 13–15,
    22, 30
Great Labor Day Hurricane, 19, 47, 64,
    86, 108–10
Great Miami Hurricane, 15, 101
Greta, 35
Guantanamo Naval Base, 28, 50
Guatemala, 58, 64
Guiney, J. See M. Lawrence et al.
Gulf of Mexico, 1, 6–7, 25, 34, 36, 39,
    41, 43, 51, 53, 56–59, 61, 64–69, 98

Haiti, 28, 32, 37, 51
Haines City, 34
Harvey, 66, pl. 22
Helene, 67–68, pl. 26
Hazel, 25, 152
Hebert, P. J., et al., 14, 17–19, 25, 80,
    91–92, 94, 96, 97–98
Hillsboro, Florida, 21, 93
Hispaniola, 36–37
Holmes, G. W., 9, 80, 88
Homestead, 20–21, 38, 93
Homestead Air Force Base, 125
Honduras, 22, 64
How, 24
Hugo, 2
Humberto, 57–58, 141

Hurricane, 1, 76, 85
Hurricane preparedness, 71
Hurricane watch, 72, 76
Hurricane warning, 72, 76

Illinois, 57
Indiana, 57
Indian Ocean, 1
Indian River Lagoon, 9, 15–16, 19, 27, 36, 91, 96
Inez, 12, 27, 32, 95, 153
Irene, 25, 66, 99, 152, pl. 23–25
Iris, 57–58, 141
Isabel (tropical storm), 39
Isbell, 27, 30, 95, 153
Isidore, 38, 155
Islamorada, 108
Ivan, 64

Jacksonville, 30, 34, 38–39, 48, 60, 66, 86
Jacksonville Beach, 20, 21
Jamaica, 21, 23, 28, 37
Jarrell, J. D., ix, 14. See also P. J. Hebert et al.
Jeanne, 64
Jenny, 34, 153
Jerry, 52, 57–58, 137, 141, pl. 5
Johns Hopkins University, Applied Physics Laboratory, pl. 11
Josephine, 59, 62
Juan, 27, 39, 97
Judith, 25, 152,
Jupiter, Florida, 16, 19, 21, 22, 64, 90–92

Karen, 57–58, 141
Karl, 63
Kate, 27, 39, 97, 121, 155
Keith, 39, 88, pl. 27
Kentucky, 57
Key Biscayne, 31
Key Largo, 18, 38, 46, 97,
Key West, 6, 11–14, 38, 50, 63, 86, 90–91, 93, 96–97, 142
King, 23–25, 27, 94
Klaus, 40

Lakeland, 26
Labor Day, 19
Lafayette, 43
Lake Okeechobee, 17, 21–22, 38, 86, 91, 93
Lake Worth, 51, 57
Landsea, C. W. See S. B. Goldenberg et al.
La Niña, 60, 62
Last Chance Saloon, 123
Lawrence, L., 16, 80
Lawrence, M., et al., 80, 99
L&N Railroad, 12
Ledesma, H. R. See G. A. Antonini et al.
Lee County, 12
Leeward Islands, 53
Leslie, 67–68, pl. 27, 28
Lesser Antilles, 42
Lester, 43
Lili, 60, 70, 98, Pl. 9
Long Key, 20, 92
Louisiana, 47, 97
Luis, 52, 57–58, 141

Major Hurricanes, xii, 5, 86
Manatee County, 39
Marathon, 38, 92, 97
Marco, 40, 60, 155
Marco Island, 91
Marilyn, 52, 57
Mayfield, M., xi. See also P. J. Hebert et al.
Mayo, 95
Melbourne, 1, 8–9, 20, 22, 27 30, 37–38, 40, 50, 65–66, 88, 96
Melbourne Times, 91
Melbourne Village, 54–56
Mestas-Nunez, A. B. See S. B. Goldenberg et al.
Mexico, 32, 58, 99
Mexico Beach, 39, 97, 140
Miami, 16, 21, 23, 31–32, 37–39, 42–42, 51, 86, 89–92, 94, 114
Miami Beach, 47
Miami Herald, xiii, 114
Miami Hurricane of 1926, 102–6
Miami International Airport, 43

Michelle, viii, 69, 70, pl. 31
Michigan, 66
Miller, B. I. See G. E. Dunn and B. I. Miller
Minimal Hurricane, 86
Minor Hurricane, 86
Mississippi, 3, 13, 18, 57, 63, 98
Mississippi River, 48, 58
Mitch, 62, 64, 99, pl. 16, 17
Mobile, Alabama, 12, 61, 86
Mobile home damage, 124
Monroe County, 46
Monthly Weather Review, xii, 97
Moore Haven, 21
Moran, Mrs., 16
Muskogee Wharf, 12

Naples, 20, 26, 34, 64, 67, pl. 22
Nassau, 18, 31–32, 42
National Climatic Center, 80
NASA, pl. 9
National Hurricane Center, xi–xii, 8, 32, 36, 42–43, 59, 67
Naval Research Laboratory, Monterey, Calif., pl. 12, 14, 18, 24, 26–28, 30, 31
National Weather Service, Melbourne, ix, pl. 1, 2, 5, 8, 22–24
Nebraska, 66
Newfoundland, 37, 43, 48
New Iberia, 43
New Orleans, 43, 47
New Smyrna Beach, 36
News/Sun Sentinel (Ft. Lauderdale), xiii
Nicaragua, 22, 64
Nicaraguan-Honduran Coast, 50
Noel, 57
NOAA, vii, xi–xii, 7–9, 12, 14, 66, 72, 75, 80, 88–89, 92–94, 97, pl. 10, 13, 15, 17, 21
North Atlantic, 1, 3, 6, 27, 60
North Carolina, 27, 51, 53, 66, 99
Northwestern U.S., 99
Norton, Grady, xi, 8, 19, 80, 86, 88, 92–93
Nova Scotia, 27, 34

Ocala, 34
Ochlockonee River, 48

Office of Emergency Management, 71
Ohio, 57
Okeechobee, 22
Opal, ix, 52, 57–58, 60, 98, 138–39, pl. 6–8
Orlando, 20, 26, 34, 38, 55, 68
Orlando International Airport, 55
Outer Banks, 53

Pablo, 58
Palm Bay, 54–55, 66, 135
Palm Beach, 1, 8, 15, 19, 21–22, 30, 36, 38, 41, 86, 91
Palm Beach International Airport, 43
Panacea, Florida, 35
Panama City, 18, 35–36, 37, 39, 49–58, 61–63, 69, 92, 96–98, 139–40
Panama City News Herald, xiii
Pardue, L. G. See A. L. Sugg et al.
Pasch, R. J., 80, 99. See also *L. A. Avila and R. J. Pasch; M. Lawrence et al.*
Peace River, 69
Pennsylvania, 43
Pensacola, 6, 12–14, 25, 39, 48, 56, 61, 67, 86, 89–91, 98
Perry, 25
Pineda Bar, 34
Pinellas County, 39
Plantation, 23
Plantation Key, 33, 95
Pompano, 22, 43, 96
Pompano Beach, 21, 93
Ponce de Leon Inlet, 91
Port Canaveral, 66
Port St. Joe, 34, 39, 91, 96
Puerto Rico, 31, 36–37, 42, 63, 65, 96, 99
Punta Gorda, 26, 34, 69, 89
Punta Rassa, 88
Putnam County, 60

Rabac, B., 8, 80, 88
Rahn, J. L. See G. A. Antonini et al.
Rappaport, E. N., 80
Red Cross, 17
Richmond, Florida, 21

Riehl, H. See R. H. Simpson and H. Riehl
Roof damage, 124
Roxanne, 5, 52, 58, 60

Saffir/Simpson Scale, xii, 2, 4–5, 7, 15, 51, 59, 65, 68, 85, 86
Saharan dust, 69
Sahel region, 2
Sand Key, 11, 13
San Juan, 42
Sanibel Island, 15
Santa Rosa County, 13
Sarasota, 20, 49–50, 69, 91
Sarasota County, 39
Savannah, 21, 37
Sebastian, Florida, 54
Sebastien, 58
Severe hurricanes, 5
Sheets, Robert, xi
Shell Point, 49
Simpson, R. H., xi, 4. *See also* Saffir/Simpson Scale
Simpson, R. H., and H. Riehl, 80
Sombrero Key, 94
South Carolina, 27 49, 59, 99–100
South China Sea, 1
South Pacific, 1
St. Andrews, 12, 30
St. Augustine, 30, 34, 68, 95
St. George Island, 53
St. Lucie County, 17, 19
St. Johns River, 30
St. Marks, 25, 53, 59, 88, 95, 98
Stephens, Lois, 43
Stephens, Thomas, 43
Storm surge, 76
Stuart, 22, 30, 91, 93
Sugg, A. L., 8, 31, 81
Sugg, A., et al., 9–10, 81
Suwannee County, 25
Suwannee River, 25, 67
Swan Island, 23, 33

Tallahassee, 49, 68–69, 86
Tampa, 20, 38, 40, 86, 90–91, 96, 100

Tampa Bay, 22
Tampico, 32
Tannehill, I. R., 8, 13, 18, 20, 29, 81
Tanya, 58
Tarpon Springs, 15, 91
Tavernier, 35, 94
Ten Thousand Islands, 21, 30
Tennessee, 43, 57
Texas, 18, 68
Titusville, 34, 42
Tornado, 99
Tropical cyclone, xii, 1, 76
Tropical depression, disturbance, 77
Tropical Prediction Center. *See* National Hurricane Center
Tropical storm warning, watch, wave, 77
Turkey Point nuclear power plants, 43, 46, 49
Typhoon, 1

University of Miami, xi
University of Michigan, pl. 29, 32
U.S. Army and Marine Hospital Docks, 11
U.S. Army Corps of Engineers, 17, 35, 42–43, 46, 81
U.S. Department of Agriculture Weather Bureau, 7
U.S. Signal Service, 7
U.S. Weather Bureau, ix, xi, 12–17, 19–22, 27, 30–31, 39, 81, 89–95, 98

Valparaiso, Florida, 14, 89
Venice, Florida, 39, 69, 88
Vero Beach, 8, 19, 30, 38, 42, 54, 96
Virginia, 49
Virginia Key, 50
Volusia County, 36, 50, 69
Vortex, 9

Wall cloud, 2
Walton County, 61
Warner, Mrs. Ruth, 16
Washington County, 12
Weatherwise magazine, 70
West African coast, 52

Western Pacific Ocean, 1
West Indies, 6, 7
West Melbourne, 55
West Palm Beach, 9, 93
West Virginia, 57
Wewahitchka, 25
Withlacoochee River, 48
Willy-willies, 1
Williams, John, 23, 28, 31–32, 54, 127, 132

Witiw, Mike, pl. 3, 6, 7
World War II, 7

Yanaros, J., 19, 81
Yankee Hurricane, 19, 92
Yankeetown, 23
Yucatan, 14, 24, 48, 53, 58, 64, 98, 99, 100
Yucatan Channel, 14, 48, 53

John M. Williams is associate faculty for hurricane research in the Department of Marine and Environmental Systems (DMES) at Florida Institute of Technology in Melbourne. While serving in the U.S. Army, he was a member of the Atmospheric Sciences Laboratory at White Sands Missile Range, where he was a staff officer specializing in satellite and radar meteorology and tropical meteorology. Before retiring from the army he was assigned to the National Hurricane Center in Coral Cables, Florida.

Iver W. Duedall is professor of oceanography and environmental science at DMES. His primary interests include chemical oceanography, pollution processes, and ocean management. Prior to coming to the Florida Institute of Technology, he was on the faculty at the State University of New York at Stony Brook.